In Old Paris

In Old Paris

An Anthology of Source Descriptions

1323–1790

Edited & Translated
by
Robert W. Berger

Italica Press
New York
2002

ITALICA PRESS, INC.
595 MAIN STREET
NEW YORK, NEW YORK 10044

LIBRARY OF CONGRESS CATALOGING-IN-PUBLICATION DATA

In old Paris : an anthology of source descriptions, 1323-1790 / edited & translated by Robert W. Berger.
p. cm.
Includes bibliographical references and index.
ISBN 0-934977-66-6 (alk. paper)
1. Paris (France)--Description and travel--Early works to 1800. I. Berger, Robert W.

DC707.I517 2002
944'.36--dc21 2001051650

Printed in the United States of America
5 4 3 2 1

Cover Art: Map of Paris from *Civitates orbis terrarum* by Georg Braun and Frans Hogenberg, Vol. I, no. 7, 1572.

About the Editor

Robert W. Berger (Ph.D. in Fine Arts, Harvard University) has taught at Brandeis University (chairman, 1975-77), and has been a visiting professor at Brown University, The Pennsylvania State University, and the University of Virginia. He has published extensively on French art and architecture in the period of Louis XIV.

Also by Robert W. Berger:

Antoine Le Pautre: A French Architect of the Era of Louis XIV

Versailles: The Château of Louis XIV

In the Garden of the Sun King: Studies on the Park of Versailles under Louis XIV

The Palace of the Sun: The Louvre of Louis XIV

A Royal Passion: Louis XIV as Patron of Architecture

Public Access to Art in Paris: A Documentary History from the Middle Ages to 1800

For Nina Rose

& Louise

CONTENTS

INTRODUCTION

Le vieux Paris n'est plus (la forme d'une ville
Change plus vite, hélas! que le coeur d'un mortel)

Old Paris is no more (the shape of a city
Changes more quickly, alas! than the human heart)

Charles Baudelaire[1]

Old Paris, the Paris that was changed forever by the political upheaval of the French Revolution during the last decade of the eighteenth century and by the physical transformation of the city under Baron Haussmann in the mid-nineteenth, survives in many architectural monuments. Some, despite all vicissitudes, are well preserved, like Notre-Dame Cathedral, the Place des Vosges, and the Invalides. Yet no matter how intact they may be, the buildings, public squares, and streets that survive from Old Paris lack the human beings who formerly inhabited and animated them. The old architecture remains mute testimony to vanished times.

A city, however, is much more than the sum of its buildings, squares, and streets. It is a locus of intense human activity played out over time in many different patterns.

[1] From "Le Cygne" (*Les Fleurs du Mal*, published 1857).

That activity, taking place within the architectural matrix of the city, is what defines the urban experience, with its special sights, sounds, and textures.

In an absolute sense, we can never re-enter medieval Paris or the Paris of Henry IV or Louis XIV (to refer to the monuments mentioned above). But the changing past appearance and life of a city can, to some extent, be restored by the written word. In the case of Paris, there is a wealth of descriptive sources, ranging in time from the Middle Ages onward and preserved in many different genres of writing. It is a fascinating body of material, which tells us much about the evolving city as well as something about the authors and their eras.

The five descriptions of Paris which comprise this anthology span four hundred and sixty-seven years of that great city's history. They were written by a diverse group of individuals: a philosophy professor at the University of Paris (the only Frenchman); a Fleming who was a professional scribe and book-dealer; the secretary to a Venetian ambassador; the important Italo-French author Marana; and the Russian writer Karamzin, who was to achieve great celebrity after his sojourn. These men were in Paris for a variety of reasons and for varying lengths of time; only Karamzin was a tourist.

The selections date from each of five consecutive centuries (fourteenth through eighteenth) and have been chosen because, in my estimation, they are the most interesting and vivid descriptions of the city from each of those centuries that are suitable for an anthology. Only Karamzin has been rendered previously into English; the others appear here in my translations. The five selections form the first such anthology on Paris in any language.

INTRODUCTION

By the early fourteenth century, the point in time when this anthology begins, Paris had already (at least a hundred years earlier) achieved its status as Europe's most populous city and the seat of the French monarchy and French cultural and intellectual life. It was also a major religious, commercial, and artistic center. It was there, during the time span of this book, that some of the greatest dramas in French history were played out, such as the English occupation at the end of the Hundred Years War, the Saint Bartholomew's Day Massacre, the Fronde, and, of course, the French Revolution. Glimpses into some of these aspects of the Parisian experience will be found in the writings themselves, but the history of the city is, understandably, beyond the scope of this book, and must be pursued elsewhere by the interested reader. (See "Parisian History, Urbanism, and Architecture: A Select Bibliography," pp. 149–50, below).

All five authors attempted to create portraits of Paris, each in his own way. A large city is an enormously complex physical and social organism, and its multifaceted character has led writers to adopt a variety of descriptive approaches or genres. Discussions of some of these are found in each of the five introductory sections, although the selections illustrate only a limited number of such genres. My main objective has been to explore literary strategies of urban description. This, it seems to me, is an under-researched field of study, and I hope that the selections included in this anthology and my analyses of the authors' varied approaches will stimulate further work in this area, whether the chosen city be Paris, London, New York, Tokyo or ______________ [fill in the blank].

IN OLD PARIS

I
JEAN DE JANDUN

A Treatise of the Praises of Paris[1]

1323

Introduction

Our writer was born probably between 1285 and 1289 in the village of Jandun in Champagne. He studied at the University of Paris, earned the Master of Arts degree there in 1310, and by 1315 was a professor (*magister artium*), teaching philosophy in the newly-founded College of Navarre, one of the schools of the university. Jean's numerous writings, which directly stemmed from his teaching, include a treatise on metaphysics and commentaries on Aristotle and Averroës; he is considered a follower of the latter philosopher. In 1316 Pope John XXII, in response to a plea from the university, promised benefices to a number of faculty, one of whom was Jean de Jandun, who was to receive a canonry in Senlis, a town north of Paris. It was there in 1323 that Jean (now finally in possession of the benefice) composed the *Tractatus de Laudibus Parisius.* He was back

[1] Extracts from *Tractatus de Laudibus Parisius.* Latin text with French translation in Antoine-Jean-Victor Le Roux de Lincy and Lazare-Maurice Tisserand, *Paris et ses historiens aux XIVe et XVe siècles* (Paris: Imprimerie Impériale, 1867), pp. 44–63 (with extensive notes).

in Paris the following year, when he took a lifetime lease on a house in the Rue Cloître-Saint-Benoît (Left Bank) along with Nicolas de Vienne, a royal civil-servant.

At the university Jean had befriended the philosopher Marsilius of Padua, rector of the university for several months in 1313. For many centuries it was believed that Jean had collaborated with Marsilius in composing a Latin tract, *Defensor Pacis* (*The Defender of Peace*), which appeared in 1324, but modern scholarship tends to regard Jean as a friend who probably contributed advice and assistance only. Called "the most original political treatise of the Middle Ages" by modern historians, *Defensor Pacis* argued that all power, spiritual and temporal, ultimately resides with the people; that princes are delegates of the people; that the pope has only spiritual, not temporal power; and that the Church should be governed by councils. The book was dedicated to King Ludwig IV of Bavaria, who was engaged in a dispute with the papacy about his powers in Germany and northern Italy.

In 1326 (three years after the composition of the *Tractatus* and two years after the appearance of *Defensor Pacis*), Marsilius was publicly connected with the latter and fled Paris, along with Jean de Jandun. The reasons for this flight are conjectural, but it is highly likely that the friends anticipated papal condemnation of the *Defensor,* along with its French translation (lost), rumored to have been prepared by Jean de Jandun. The two professors hurried to Nuremberg, finding refuge at the court of King Ludwig. One year later, in 1327, John XXII issued a bull pronouncing *Defensor Pacis* a heretical book, and condemned Marsilius and Jean as heretics.

In 1328 Ludwig marched on Rome and was crowned Holy Roman Emperor. He declared Pope John (who was sitting on the papal throne in Avignon) deposed and installed an antipope, Nicholas V. These dramatic events were orchestrated by Marsilius, thus putting into practice the tenets of the *Defensor.* Throughout this episode, Jean de Jandun was at Ludwig's side as an adviser. The emperor rewarded Jean by naming him bishop of Ferrara in that same year, a direct application of a principle found in *Defensor Pacis* (appointment of a bishop by the temporal ruler, the people, and the clergy, but not by the pope). This elevation, however, could not be effectuated, and Jean was named instead the emperor's secretary and a member of his household. But Ludwig was forced to abandon Rome in August 1328 because of the displeasure of the Roman people; Jean de Jandun died the next month in Montalto, as Ludwig and his entourage were retreating to Pisa.

The *Tractatus de Laudibus Parisius* has come down to us in only two manuscripts (Paris, Bibliothèque Nationale de France, Département des manuscrits, ms. latin 14884; and Vienna, Biblioteca Augusta Palatina, no. 4753); its Latin style has been described as "pretentious, obscure, and rather barbarous." The author begins by extolling the University of Paris and its various faculties, then moves to the material that concerns us — the praise and description of the city of Paris (excerpts given below) — and concludes with sections dealing with the French king, another with a personal detractor, and a final one in praise of the town of Senlis, whose provincial charms form a contrast with Paris.

As we might expect from a medieval writer, the encomium of Paris begins with an estimation and description of the largest and most important church of the city, Notre-Dame, then moves to the king's chapel, the Sainte-Chapelle. The descriptions combine aesthetic sensitivity with religious enthusiasm, and this entire first chapter ends with praises of these sanctuaries, the hymns sung within them, and the Masses celebrated on their altars. Although Jean then proceeds to the secular features of Paris, a religious sensibility pervades his writing, as when he says of the inhabitants that their feeling of civic security — due to the abundance of arms in the city — "does not prevent them from placing before their eyes the rampart of Divine Power" (Chapter IV). And the epilogue (Chapter IX) to the chapters on Paris is a prayer for the prosperity of the city.

After Notre-Dame and the Sainte-Chapelle, the third most important building in the mind of Jean de Jandun is the Palace, the king's residence at the western end of the Île de la Cité, the secular counterweight to Notre-Dame at the east end. The famous statues of French kings and the marble table are described, but Jean's main interest is the activity of the officials and judges who carry out the administrative and legal work of government there, making "public matters prosper" and absolving the innocent and punishing the guilty. The author then turns to the commercial and economic activity of the city (Chapter III), giving a detailed account of the Halles des Champeaux (the great market on the Right Bank, precursor of the later Halles Centrales), which includes perhaps the earliest description anywhere of the behavior of the shopper: scouring the ranges of booths and then succumbing to "an insatiable fervor to renew this pleasure."

Specific items of merchandise are mentioned in this chapter, such as draperies, animal skins, silks, clothing, ivory combs, mirrors, belts, purses, gloves, necklaces, and wedding and festival decorations. The impression is of an entrepôt of luxury goods — a characteristic of Paris from that time to the present.

In Chapter IV the author enlarges his description of Paris as an economic forum with an enumeration of its manual artisans, "without whom the integrity of the political order is not complete." These include image-makers (sculptors and painters), makers of armaments and "objects necessary for horsemen," fabricators of clothing and ornaments, bakers, metal-vase makers, and all those connected with the booktrade: parchment-makers, scribes, illuminators, and binders.

After some comments on the moral and physical qualities of the citizenry (including two themes that reappear in later writings — the liveliness of the Parisians and the French, and the unfaithfulness of some of the married women), Jean returns to the economy of the city, recognizing the Seine as the economic highway that brings food and provisions to the fertile basin of Paris, the Terrestrial Paradise.

Upon analysis, then, this encomium, which begins with enthusiastic Christian descriptions of churches and ends with a prayer to God, turns out to be precocious, at least in the Parisian context, in its recognition of the vital importance of the economic components and activity of a city. Not surprisingly, we shall encounter this theme in later writers, but Jean de Jandun must be acknowledged as the earliest writer on Paris to discuss it.

In a broad sense the *Tractatus de Laudibus Parisius* belongs to the *laudes* (praises) tradition of city descriptions. In this genre of writing — usually due to a native or adopted son, rather than to a visitor — a city is extolled to the heavens for its natural setting, the magnificence of its buildings, the excellence of its citizens, the beauty of its women, etc., etc. Such writings, found in ancient Greek and Roman sources, reappeared from the early Middle Ages on in Italy, and only later in northern Europe. A few descriptive encomiums of Paris are found long before Jean de Jandun: near the beginning of the poem (written between 888 and 897) by the monk Abbo of Saint-Germain-des-Prés on the Norman siege of the city in 885–86; in a letter by the monk Gui de Bazoches (c. 1175); and, more vaguely, in the poem "Architrenius" (1184) by Johannes de Hauvilla (Jean de Hauteville). But Jean de Jandun's "Treatise," written at a moment when the mature medieval city of Paris had already come into being, stands apart from these early examples by its length and wealth of detail. Although part of a larger compendium, it looks ahead to the independent prose descriptions and guidebooks of Paris of much later times.

When Jean — an adopted Parisian from a tiny provincial village — wrote his "Treatise" in 1323 and entered into a lifetime lease on a house in the city the following year, he surely was looking forward with confidence to spending his remaining days in the intellectual capital of Europe. But he fell victim to unexpected events, and his precipitous flight in 1326 removed him from his beloved city, which he would never see again.

BIBLIOGRAPHY

Ludwig Schmugge, *Johannes von Jandun (1285/89–1328)* (Stuttgart: Anton Hiersemann, 1966). On the question of his collaboration with Marsilius of Padua, see Alan Gewirth, "John of Jandun and the *Defensor Pacis*," *Speculum* 23 (1948): 267–72; and Schmugge, *op. cit.*, pp. 118-19. The *Tractatus de Laudibus Parisius* is briefly discussed by John Kenneth Hyde, "Medieval Descriptions of Cities," *Bulletin of the John Rylands Library* 48 (1966): 333; this important article (pp. 308-340) gives a survey and bibliography of medieval descriptions of Italian, French, and English cities from c. 738 to 1340.

A Treatise of the Praises of Paris

Chapter I

Of the Churches, Mainly Notre-Dame and the Royal Chapel [the Sainte-Chapelle]

In Paris, privileged sanctuary of the Christian religion, some beautiful edifices consecrated to God have been founded in such great quantity that there probably are not many cities among the most powerful of Christendom that can boast to number as many houses of God. Among these palaces, the imposing church of the very glorious Virgin Mary, mother of God, shines in the first rank, and deservedly so, like the sun in the midst of the other stars. And although certain people, by the freedom of their estimation (but who are only able to easily see a few objects), maintain that the beauty of some other churches prevails over this one, I think, with all due respect, that if they would examine it attentively in its entirety and in its details they would soon abandon that opinion. Where is to be found, I ask you, two towers of such magnificence, as perfect, as high, as wide, as strong, enriched with such variety, such multiplicity of ornaments? Where is to be encountered, pray tell, such a complex series of lateral vaults, low as well as high? Where is to be found, I repeat, the bright splendor of such a belt of chapels? This is not all: tell me in what church I shall see a cross of similar size, one arm of which separates the choir from the nave? Finally, I would be pleased to hear: where would I be able to see two similar rose windows mutually facing one another in a straight line, roses to which the name of the fourth vowel [O] has been given because of their resemblance to it? Below, smaller roses, *rosaces,* arranged with marvelous art, some circular, others lozenge-shaped, surround sparkling stained glass embellished with precious colors and with figures painted with the most exquisite delicacy. In truth, I think that this church offers to those who carefully look at it such an admirable object that the soul has difficulty satisfying itself while contemplating it.

But the most beautiful of chapels, the king's chapel [the Sainte-Chapelle], very conveniently placed within the perimeter of the royal residence, is admired for its very strong structure and for the indestructible solidity of the materials that form it. The carefully chosen colors of its paintings, the precious gilding of its images, the pure transparency of the stained glass that shines on all sides, the rich adornments of its altars, the marvelous virtues of its sanctuaries, the exotic ornaments of its reliquary shrines decorated with dazzling precious stones, give to that house of prayer such a degree of beauty that upon entering it one believes oneself carried up to the heavens, and one with reason believes oneself to be introduced into one of the most beautiful rooms of paradise.

Oh! How salutary are the prayers that rise from these sanctuaries toward God the all-powerful, when the interior purity of the spirits of the faithful exactly responds to the material and external ornaments of the oratories!

Oh! How sweet are the praises of the most merciful God, chanted in these tabernacles, when the hearts of those who chant them are embellished with virtues in harmony with the beautiful paintings of the tabernacles!

Oh! How pleasing to the most glorious God are the sacrifices prepared on these altars, when the lives of the sacrificers shine with a lustre equal to the gold of the altars!

CHAPTER II

OF THE PALACE OF THE KING, WHEREIN ARE DISCUSSED THE MASTERS OF PARLEMENT, THE MASTERS OF PETITIONS, AND THE ROYAL NOTARIES

In this very famous seat of the French monarchy, a splendid Palace has been built, superb testimony of royal magnificence. Its impregnable walls offer among themselves an enclosure sufficiently vast and extensive as to be able to contain a countless multitude. In honor of their glorious memory, statues of all the kings of France who up to now have occupied the throne are reunited in this place. Their resemblance is so expressive that at first sight one would believe them to be living. The marble table, whose uniform surface offers the most brilliant polish, is placed at the west, under the reflection of the stained-glass windows, in such a manner that the guests are turned toward the east; it is of such a size that, were I to cite its dimensions without giving proof, I would fear that I would not be believed.

The Palace of the king has been decorated neither for indolence and the gross pleasures of the senses, nor erected in order to flatter the false and deceitful vanity of vainglory, nor fortified in order to shelter the perfidious plots of a proud tyranny; but it has been marvelously adapted to the active, effective, and complete attentions of the prudence of our kings, who untiringly seek by their decrees to increase the public good. Indeed, on the elevated seats that appear on both sides of the hall, one sees seated almost every day government officials who are called, according to their proper functions, some masters of petitions, the others notaries of the king. All, according to their rank, obedient to royal orders, labor to make public matters prosper: it is from them that emanate, almost incessantly, the benevolent and honorable favors of pardons; it is by them that are presented the petitions, weighed with the most sincere scales of equity.

In a vast and beautiful chamber to which a special door gives access, built into the north wall of the hall (because the difficult matters dealt with there demand a greater tranquillity and a more complete seclusion), men of ever-alert competency sit in their court; they are called the masters of Parlement. Their infallible knowledge of law and customs allows them to discuss cases with full wisdom and leniency, and to hurl the thunderbolts of their final sentences, which give transports of joy to the innocent and just, because they are rendered without regard to persons or gifts, in the contemplation of God alone and the law. But the wicked and the impious, to the extent of their iniquity, are overwhelmed with grief and misfortune.

CHAPTER III

OF THE HALLES DES CHAMPEAUX AND THE OTHER HOUSES OF PARIS

This joyful abode of the most pleasing diversions offers, in the form of very large displays full of inestimable treasures, all the most varied sorts of precious objects brought together in the building called the Halles des Champeaux. There, if you have the desire and the means, you will be able to buy all the types of ornaments that the most practiced industry and the most inventive spirit hasten to imagine to gratify all your desires. To wish to describe in their details all the specialties that these types include would be to protract this work and give it such a length that it would give rise to boredom in the reader's soul and would show him how the author forgets himself when he attempts impossible things. I do not wish, however, to omit entirely to say that, in some places amid the lower parts of this market, and as it were beneath some heaps, some piles of other merchandise, are found draperies, one more beautiful than the other; in others, some superb pelisses, some made of animal skins, others of silk materials, others, finally, composed of delicate and foreign materials, whose Latin names I confess not to know. In the upper part of the building, which is formed like a street of an astonishing length, are displayed all the objects that serve to adorn the different parts of the human body: for the head, crowns, braids, caps; ivory combs for the hair; mirrors for looking at oneself; belts for the loins; purses to hang at the side; gloves for the hands; necklaces for the breast; and other things of this sort that I cannot cite, rather because of the penury of Latin words than for not having actually seen them. But, in order that the splendors without number of these brilliant objects — whose varieties and infinite number stand in the way of a complete and detailed description — may at least be touched upon in a superficial summary, allow me to speak to you thus: in these places of display, the strollers' gazes see smiling in their eyes so many decorations for wedding and great festival entertainments, that, after having half-scoured one range, an impetuous desire carries them to the other, and after having traversed the entire length, an insatiable fervor to renew this pleasure — not once nor twice, but almost indefinitely, in returning to the beginning — makes them recommence the excursion, if they wished to follow their desire.

I have said enough about the building called the Halles des Champeaux. But he who would count the number of other houses in Paris would probably labor in vain, rather like the one who would try to count the hairs of several abundantly furnished heads, or the ears of corn of a great harvest, or the leaves of a great forest. How many great and beautiful houses of the rich and famous! Some are those of kings, counts, dukes, knights, and other barons; others belong to prelates; all are numerous, grand, well-built, beautiful, and splendid, to the point that by themselves and separated from the other houses, they could constitute a marvelous city.

CHAPTER IV

OF THE MANUAL ARTISANS

It seems to us good, if this survey does not displease you, to add here some remarks concerning the manual artisans. Let us say then that the manual artisans (without whom the integrity of the political order is not complete), in the center of that so abundant ensemble of all the necessary elements, crowd together in a neighborhood so close together and in such a number that the eyes, surveying all the streets, cannot find two contiguous houses that are not more or less peopled by them. And in order to group under several main headings the different types of industries that cannot be described in detail, may it be permitted for us to speak thus: in Paris are found very skilled image-makers, be it in sculpture, in painting, in relief; there you will see ingenious artificers of instruments of war and even of all the objects necessary for horsemen: saddles and bits, swords and shields, lances and javelins, bows and cross-bows, mallets and arrows, cuirasses and metal plates, iron caps and helmets; in short, to be brief, all the weapons suitable for attack and defense are found in such number in that quiet abode of security, that they can frighten the fierce spirit of enemies and banish all fear from the hearts of the loyal inhabitants, which does not prevent them from placing before their eyes the rampart of Divine Power. You will also find there men who fabricate clothing and ornaments with very great care.

As for the bakers, it is not out of place to say here that they are themselves gifted with an astonishing superiority in their art above all the other workers of this sort, or that the materials that they use, namely grain and water, are so much preferable to others that, for this reason, the bread that they make acquires an unbelievable degree of goodness and delicacy. It is better still that these two qualities are united. Also are to be found, on the Grand-Pont and in many other locations, excellent sculptors of metal vases, principally of gold and silver, tin and copper, according to the facility of each, making the hammers resound on the anvils, forming as it were a harmonious cadence. There are also the parchment-makers, the scribes, the illuminators, and the binders, who labor with so much the more ardor in decorating the works of knowledge of which they are the servants, that they see flowing with greater abundance the smiling fountains of human knowledge, spouting forth from that inexhaustible spring of all goodness. As for the other types of manual workers, either because they are sufficiently known, or because I fear prolixity, I shall say nothing about them, not wishing to prolong this discourse.

CHAPTER V

OF THE MORAL AND PHYSICAL CONDITIONS OF THE PARISIAN PEOPLE

In preparing myself to describe the moral and physical character of the citizens of Paris, it has seemed to me that many of those who were born in Paris of an ancient family are gifted with such moderation and such gentleness that, by a praiseworthy propensity, they have little inclination to fly into a passion; but those among them who stray from the straight and narrow sin rather by outbursts rather than by apathy. The majority among them appear pleasant by their charming affability, their urbanity, and the gentleness of their spirit; but those among them who do not hold to the golden mean appear sooner calm than insolent. Most of the Parisians, and the French in general, are remarkably lively; but if they deviate to one side or the other, they fall rather into buffoonery than into simplicity, through absence of a proper education. The Parisian people are for the most part honest and open; but those who do not keep to the straight path can become sometimes a bit too boastful. The stature of Parisians does not reach down to the contemptible diminutiveness of dwarfs; but also their bodies do not languish under the weight of a gigantic mass. Their limbs have neither the brutal and servile coarseness of an athlete like Milo, nor the softness and elasticity of female flesh; but they are endowed with a medium stature, with a very fine presence, qualities that are no less accompanied, as befits free men, with the vigor necessary for civil life and the toils of war.

So much for the men. What to say now about the women? I like to believe that the wives and mothers of families — notwithstanding the luxury and excessive variety of their attire, and despite the ineffable beauties of their faces — preserve the laws of marriage, and that, thanks to God, they shall preserve them beyond all attack. If however some among them, chaining their husbands to the inconstant belt of the cunning Venus, have shamefully astonished the religion of a wise man, I beg the very-merciful God — who alone can render pure that which is not — to restore them to the path of salvation.

CHAPTER VI

OF THE RIVER THAT PASSES THROUGH PARIS AND IS CALLED THE SEINE

In this fertile basin of Paris, which seems to have received from the Almighty the role of Terrestrial Paradise, a justly famous river, named the Seine, arrives to spread itself out. The sufficient breadth of its bed, the moderate speed of its flow, not impetuous but tranquil, furnish in abundance the riches from all parts of the world necessary for men's needs. The Seine furnishes in great number the wines of Greece, Grenache, La Rochelle, Gascony, and Burgundy; it brings in quantity wheat, rye, peas, beans, hay, oats, salt, charcoal, and wood.

CHAPTER VII

OF FOOD AND PROVISIONS

A great weight would certainly crush my weak shoulders if all the sorts of foods were worthy of occupying by their proper names distinct places in this work. Who will indeed enumerate the diverse types of animals of the land, sea, and air, the varieties of plants, fruits, vegetables, which, boiled or roasted, are suitable for the nourishment of man? I think it suffices for the moment to say that this city is supplied at any time with provisions so varied and so fine that a palate aroused by hunger will never be deprived of satisfying itself with simple or choice foods. But the sale and purchase prices of these products are subject to the variations in price that opportunity or the difficulty of the times command. What seems marvelous is that it often happens that the more the multitude abounds in Paris, the more is supplied a superabundant number, a numerous superabundance of foodstuffs, without there being produced a proportional increase in the price of provisions.

Jean de Jandun

Chapter IX

In Which in Form of an Epilogue Is Found: An Exclamative Résumé for the Famous City of Paris

Returning therefore to our subject and summing up in a short chapter some motifs of praise, we say: may it grow proud in the Lord, may all men of good will glorify it, this fortunate place, which sees live and grow so many types of wise men, from whose lips, like the partly-open flanks of high mountains, salutary doctrines shoot forth and are spread throughout the world, in the same way as the inexhaustible waves of beneficent rivers! May it tremble in the Lord, and may all men of good will celebrate it, this holy place whose inhabitants adore the glory of the Savior in such a great number of vast and beautiful oratories! May it rejoice in the Lord, and may it be praised by all men of good will, this fecund place embellished by the course of a river which is neither frightful nor impetuous, but pleasant and tranquil. May it be pleased in the Lord, and may it be admired by all men of good will, this favorable place, in which are the reservoirs of all the riches, to the degree that the ensemble of its sole resources does not allow it to be deprived of any benefit, useful, pleasant, or honest! That in the plenitude of this prosperity, may this city of cities be preserved and governed by the supreme Prince, who alone, by the immense vigor of an infinite merit, directs the entire universe!

II
GUILLEBERT DE METS

THE DESCRIPTION OF THE CITY OF PARIS AND OF THE EXCELLENCE OF THE KINGDOM OF FRANCE[1]

1407–34

INTRODUCTION

Guillebert de Mets was born c. 1360 in the Flemish town of Grammont (Geraardsbergen), the son of a butcher. In that town (which lay within the duchy of Burgundy) he later held the positions of alderman *(échevin)* in 1425, communal tax collector *(receveur communal)* in 1430, and alderman again in 1434. From at least 1430 on, he was proprietor of an inn there, with the sign "l'Écu de France."

[1] Translated from "La Description de la ville de Paris et de l'excellence du royaume de France, transcript et extraict de pluseurs aucteurs par Guillebert de Mets, l'an Mil IIII^{c} et XXXIIII." French text published in Antoine-Jean-Victor Le Roux de Lincy and Lazare-Maurice Tisserand, *Paris et ses historiens aux XIVe et XVe siècles* (Paris: Imprimerie Impériale, 1867), pp. 152-234 (with extensive notes and appendixes); pp. 119-30 contain a discussion of the "Description" and reproductions of several examples of the author's scribal hand.

Guillebert was by profession a scribe and book-dealer; his scribal training was probably obtained in the local monastic school in Grammont. Several manuscripts have been recognized as his handiwork, including one with the first French translation of Boccaccio's *Decameron* (Paris, Bibliothèque de l'Arsenal, ms. 5070, signed by Guillebert and dated 1417; the translation was due to Laurent de Premierfait, whom Guillebert mentions in his final chapter). Some of the illuminations in this manuscript are by a south Netherlandish artist whom art historians have awkwardly dubbed "The Master of Guillebert de Mets." In this manuscript, Guillebert writes that he is living in Grammont at "l'Écu de France." A note added to another Guillebert manuscript states that he was bookseller *(libraire)* to Duke John of Burgundy (John the Fearless, assassinated in 1419), and this must have been while he lived in Paris, the duke's place of residence. A document of 1432 records payment for two books to Guillebert by John's successor, Duke Philip the Good. Further evidence of Guillebert's dealings in the book trade with the Burgundian dukes arises from the fact that the only known manuscript of his "Description" (Brussels, Bibliothèque Royale Albert Ier, no. 9562) came from the ducal library, as did other manuscripts attributed to his hand.

Guillebert lived in Paris from at least 1407 (perhaps earlier) to before 1417, working as a scribe and book-dealer; in the "Description" he mentions several Parisian colleagues in the scribal trade and even an otherwise unknown treatise by one of them. The "Description" was mainly written at that time in several installments and was completed in Grammont in 1434, the terminal date given in the *incipit* of the manuscript. References to Parisian events of 1418 and 1422 were probably obtained secondhand, for by then Paris was a city at war, embroiled in the final phase of the Hundred Years War and occupied by the English from 1420 to 1436.

The "Description" is composed of thirty chapters. The first nineteen contain material on the early history of France, lifted almost verbatim from earlier sources. But in Chapters XX-XXX, Guillebert comes into his own, describing the Paris he knew from direct experience.

For the first time in writings on Paris, a topographical approach is used to organize the material. This is spelled out at the beginning of Chapter XX, where Guillebert tells us that he will describe, in the following order: the Île de la Cité, the Left Bank, the Right Bank, and the defensive perimeter, which contains the city gates. Then there will be a final chapter on the excellence of Paris.

This method looks ahead, precociously, to the later guidebooks on Paris of the seventeenth and eighteenth centuries, as does Guillebert's desire to mention as many monuments and streets as he can, sometimes enumerating them in simple lists. He occasionally gives measurements of buildings (erroneous in the case of Notre-Dame) or enumerates objects for the sake of "completeness," as when he mentions that the Sainte-Chapelle contains the Crown of Thorns as well as the foot of a griffon. Piquant details do not escape him, like the tin-potter at the Palace who keeps nightingales that sing in winter, the double spiral-stairs at the Petit-Châtelet and the Bernardins that allow people to mount or descend without seeing one another, and the tower that a man had constructed over his grave at the Innocents Cemetery "so that he could boast during his lifetime that the dogs would not piss on his grave." In such instances Guillebert foreshadows the cicerone of later times, who will insert such details to entertain and hold his audience.

Surprisingly detailed and a treasure for architectural, social, and economic historians is Guillebert's description of the interior of the Hôtel of Master Jacques Duchié, a wealthy clerk in the Chambre des Comptes (the royal exchequer) of Charles VI. This house stood on the Right Bank, and a fragment of its street, the Rue de Prouvelles, survives as the Rue des Prouvaires. Guillebert obviously had been admitted to this building, raising the possibility that Jacques Duchié (whose books in his chapel are mentioned by Guillebert) was his patron.

"Data" concerning the number of wine taverns, beggars, scribes (more than 60,000! — surely a gross exaggeration), and the weekly consumption of wine and meat are given in the last chapter, continuing the writer's predilection for statistics and enumeration. But whereas (in striking contrast to Jean de Jandun) he reveals no religious emotion when describing Notre-Dame and the Sainte-Chapelle, he does at times betray a feeling of a special sort — nostalgia. For Guillebert tells us that "Paris was in its flower" in the year 1400 — seven years before his "Description" begins — leading us to believe that he was in the city as early as that date. And in the final chapter he enumerates (in the imperfect indicative tense) the many distinguished individuals who contributed to that flowering, citing most of them by name, and including "three brothers, manuscript illuminators" (Pol, Herman, and Jean Limbourg), his colleague, the scribe (and alchemist) Nicolas Flamel, and the proto-feminist writer Christine de Pisan. Some anonymous beauties are also listed: *la Belle Saunière* (the beautiful salt-merchant's wife), *la Belle Bouchière* (the beautiful butcher's wife), *la Belle Charpentière* (the beautiful carpenter's wife), *la Belle Herbière* (the beautiful herb-woman), "and the one they simply called Belle."

Guillebert's nostalgia for the Paris of not many years previous — although in the popular medieval literary tradition of *ubi sunt* — surely reflects the dangerous and disordered times in which he wrote. For in 1407, when he began composing the "Description," John the Fearless, duke of Burgundy (cousin to the intermittently mad French king, Charles VI) had his rival for power, Louis, duke of Orléans (the king's brother) assassinated. This act ignited a civil war between two factions, the Burgundians and the Orléanist allies, known as the Armagnacs. Fighting began in 1411, followed by a massacre of Armagnacs by the Burgundians in Paris in 1413. In 1415, King Henry V of England, sensing opportunity, invaded France and annihilated the French army at Agincourt. After the assassination of John the Fearless, arranged by the French Dauphin (later Charles VII) in 1419, the Burgundians allied themselves with the English, who took control of Paris in 1420, remaining masters of the city until 1436.

As noted above, Guillebert was back in Grammont by 1417, but while living in Paris he had witnessed the early years of the struggle between Burgundians, Armagnacs, and English, which made life in the city so difficult, as documented in a remarkable diary kept at the time by an anonymous cleric, the so-called *Journal d'un bourgeois de Paris,* covering the years 1405-49. Guillebert ends the "Description" on a lugubrious note, reporting on the great epidemic of 1418 (corroborated by the *Journal)* and the delivery of burial shrouds for more than 30,000 corpses (information that must have reached him second-hand in Flanders). No wonder the year 1400 seemed to him like Paris's Golden Age!

Bibliography

Victor Fris, "Guillebert de Mets," *Annales de l'Académie royale d'archéologie de Belgique* 64 (1912): 333-66. Nicole Grévy-Pons, "Jean de Montreuil et Guillebert de Mets," *Revue belge de philologie et d'histoire* 58.3 (1980): 565-87.

The Description of the City of Paris and of the Excellence of the Kingdom of France

XX

There Follows the Description of the City of Paris in the Year 1407, which Description is Divided into Five Parts. The First Part Contains the Middle Section Called La Cité, between Two Arms of the River Seine. The Second Part Is of the Upper Part of the City Where the Schools of the University Are. The Third Part Speaks of the Lower Part of the City towards Saint-Denis en France. The Fourth Is of the Gates of the Entire City. The Fifth Part Discusses in General the Excellence of the City.

The First is of the Cité

There is the cathedral church of Notre-Dame, which on the inside is two hundred feet long and eighty feet wide. There are within the three first entrances,[1] forty columns that one can walk around; also there are twenty columns, each with a chapel, that one cannot walk around. Around the choir of the church are also as many columns and chapels. The space that is in the middle of the church, that is

[1] The three west façade portals.

between the choir and the entrance, contains as much space as twelve columns; and there are six chapels. Around the choir are sculpted in stone the acts of the Apostles and the story of Joseph the Patriarch, a pleasant work, and Master Pierre du Coingnet.[2] At the entrance is the image of Saint Christopher, of astonishing height and noble workmanship. In this church is the head of Saint Philip the Apostle, the head of Saint Marcel, bishop of Paris, and several other relics. The table of the great altar above and that of the one below are of gilded silver. There are two bell-towers with as many steps as there are days in the year. In one is a bell that one can barely encircle four times around with arms extended. There is a side chapel, as one goes to the chapter-house, of marvelous design; the legend of Job is sculpted there. And there are beautiful images on the church exterior. Next to the church on one side is the bishop's palace: pleas are heard there before the bishop's officer and his auditors; also the master of testaments holds his court there. On the other side live the canons, and there is found the court of the ecclesiastical judge and the archdeacon. The church of Notre-Dame is an excellent work inside and out.

On the Île de la Cité are fifteen parish churches, namely:

Saint-Pierre-aux-Boeufs,
Saint-Pierre-des-Assis,
Saint-Christophe,
Sainte-Marie-Madeleine,
Sainte-Marine [etc.]

[2] A grotesque sculpture.

XXI

OF THE PALACE

The Royal Palace extends from the Grand-Pont [Pont au Change], where the clock is, to the Pont Saint-Michel. The Great Hall of the Palace is one hundred and twenty feet long by fifty feet wide; there are eight columns. There is found the marble table made of nine pieces; there are the images of the kings who have reigned in France; there are procurators of the Parlement and lawyers. The hall of the haberdashers is eighty feet long. There is sold various jewelry of gold, silver, precious stones, and other materials.

In the Sainte-Chapelle is a large part of the Holy Cross, of the Holy Crown [of Thorns], and other hallowed, wonderful relics. And there is a large foot of a griffon.

In the Palace are halls and rooms to lodge the king and the twelve peers. It is a handsome building with towers and images inside and out; and there is a beautiful garden. In the Palace are the lords of the Parlement and where the French kings are accustomed to sit in judgment. There are found the masters of petitions, who have knowledge of the trials of the king's officers. There is found the chamber of the lords of the accounts, of the treasurers, of the receivers, of the concierge, and of other officers. There is found the tribunal. And in front of the Palace resides a tinpotter, a good artisan of marvelous tin vessels; and he keeps nightingales who sing in winter.

The great hospital [Hôtel-Dieu], founded by King Saint Louis, extends from the church of Notre-Dame to the Petit-Pont. There are in front of the hospital, in the Rue Neuve, thirty-seven houses with a butcher-shop and an empty square in front of the chapel of the hospital.

XXII

Of the Bridges

The Grand-Pont [Pont au Change] has on one side sixty-eight rented shops and on the other, seventy-two; the money-changers reside on one side and the goldsmiths on the other. In the year 1400, when the city was in its flower, so many people passed all day long on this bridge that one immediately encountered a white monk [a Carmelite] or a white horse.

The Pont Notre-Dame: there are found beautiful houses. There are sixty-four that belong to the city and eighteen owned by various persons. In 1422 five more houses were begun, when this description was made.

The Petit-Pont is very strong, and is made from the foundation up of large slats attached together with iron and lead. The Petit-Châtelet is there, with a wall so thick that they can manage a cart on top of it. There are beautiful gardens above these walls; there is a double spiral-stair, in which those who mount by one way do not see the others who come down by the other.

The Pont Saint-Michel is well appointed with houses....

XXIII

In the Upper Part of the City Where the Schools Are

The parish church of Saints Peter and Paul, which is called Sainte-Geneviève.... The abbey of the canons regular of Sainte-Geneviève, where pleas are argued before the abbot of cases that the pope has dismissed. Here is the chancellery of the university; and it is proper that the chancellor belongs to the order of this abbey. The abbot holds high, middle, and low justice. Also the church holds such prerogative that no patriarch, archbishop, or bishop may enter in their proper habit, but in the habit of canon.

Item: there is a crypt beneath the central part of the choir where there are the sepulchers of Saint Geneviève and other saints.

Item: in the third lower part of the choir where the canons chant are the tombs of King Clovis, the first Christian king who founded this church, and the Queen Saint Clotilde, his wife. At the college of the Bernardins is a church, a very beautiful and high edifice; and there is a marvelous spiral-stair, which has a double set of steps, so that those who mount or descend by one of the stairs are unaware of others who move about on the other stair. The church of the Mathurins, where the rector holds his sitting, as well as the conservator and the chancellor's judge. Also the assemblies of the entire university are held here....

Item: many teachers and a great number of students.

Item: near the Petit-Pont are sold poultry, eggs, game, and other foodstuffs; and in the Place Maubert, bread. The walls of the city are very strong and thick, so that a cart can be driven on top of them. On the Île Notre-Dame [Île Saint-Louis] are palisades for fighting and bowers for shooting with the crossbow and bow....

XXIV

IN THE LOWER PART OF THE CITY, SHORT OF THE BRIDGES

...At Sainte-Catherine is the Sepulcher of Our Lord in such form as it is in Jerusalem; and in that church is the image of Bertrand Du Guesclin such as he was accustomed to be in his lifetime.

At the Célestins is a painted Paradise and Hell [Last Judgment], with other images of noble workmanship in a separate choir.

Item: before the choir of the church at an altar is a painted image of Our Lady of sovereign mastery.

At the church of the Innocents is a complete Innocent[3] encased in gold and silver. There are, ingeniously sculpted in stone, the images of the Three Living and the Three Dead. There is found a very large cemetery, enclosed with buildings called charnel houses, where the bones of the dead are piled up. There are notable paintings of the Danse Macabre and other paintings, with inscriptions to move people to devotion. One part of the cemetery belongs to the church of the Innocents, the other part is for the great hospital, and the third part is for the churches of Paris that do not have cemeteries.

Item: in this cemetery is a small tower at the site of a tomb where there is a very well fashioned image of Our Lady carved in stone. Concerning the small tower, it is said that a man had it erected over his sepulcher so that he could boast during his lifetime that the dogs would not piss on his grave....

[3] A Christian child allegedly killed by Jews.

The Châtelet, where the Provost of Paris and his auditors hold audience; and there are an astonishing number of jail cells there.

The Hôtel de Ville [Maison aux Piliers] in the Place de Grève, where the Provost of Merchants and the magistrates make laws.

The hôtel called the For-l'Évêque, where the temporal cases in the jurisdiction of the bishop of Paris are heard; it is in the Rue de l'École-Saint-Germain.

The markets of cloths, skins, haberdashery, leather, bread, fruit, and other things take up the space of a sizable city.

In the markets near the pillory is a fountain, two in the Rue Saint-Denis and two in the Rue Saint-Martin. In the Grève is the entrepôt for wine, wood, charcoal, hay, and other merchandise from boats; there are the porters of harnesses and bundlers of hay....

XXV

THE HÔTEL OF MASTER JACQUES DUCHIÉ IN THE RUE DE PROUVELLES

Its gate is carved with marvelous skill; in the court were peacocks and various birds of pleasure. The first hall is decorated with various pictures and instructive writings attached to and hung from the walls. There is another hall filled with all sorts of instruments: harps, organs, hurdy-gurdies, citterns, psalteries and others, all of which said Master Jacques knows how to play. Another hall was adorned with chess-sets, tables, and other divers sorts of games in great number.

Item: a beautiful chapel where there were lecterns upon which to place books of marvelous art, which were brought to various seats far and near, to right and left.

Item: a study where the walls were covered with precious stones and spices of delicate odor. Item: a room where were furs of various sorts.

Item: several other rooms richly equipped with beds, with tables ingeniously carved and adorned with rich fabrics and gold-fringed carpets.

Item: in another high chamber were a great number of crossbows, some of which were painted with beautiful figures. There were found flags, banners, pennons, bows, pikes, poniards, spears, axes, hatchets, coats of mail and lead, bucklers, targes, shields, canons and other machines, with much armor; and in short there was also all sorts of war-apparatus.

Item: there was a window made with marvelous skill, from which was extended outside a hollow device of iron plates, by means of which one looked at and spoke with those outside, if it were necessary, without fear of arrows.

Item: at the very top of the house was a square chamber where there were windows on all sides to look down on the city. And when one ate there, they raised and lowered wine and meat by means of a pulley, because it was too high up to carry them. And above the gables of the house were beautiful gilded sculptures. This Master Jacques Duchié was a fine man, honest, and very distinguished. Also he had servants well brought-up and trained, of pleasing countenance, among whom was a master carpenter, who worked continually at the house. A great number of rich bourgeois had servants and officers, the latter called "little kings of grandeur."

The hôtel of Guillemin Sanguin, in the Rue des Bourdonnais, is an excellent edifice, where there are as many locks as there are days in the year. The hôtels of the bishops and prelates, of the lords of the Parlement, the lords of the Chambre des Comptes, the knights, bourgeois, and various officers are in great number. Among which is the hôtel of Sieur Mille Baillet in the Rue de la Verrerie, who was the king's treasurer; in this hôtel was a chapel where they celebrated the divine office every day. There were halls, rooms, and studies on the ground floor for living in summer, and upstairs the same arrangement for living in winter; there are as many glass windows as days in the year....

Around the Châtelet they sold salt, fruit, and herbs, and all year long they fashioned there hats of different flowers and greenery; and in front of the Châtelet was the Grande Boucherie. In front of the hôtel of the admiral,[4] near Saint-Jean[-en-Grève], was a bizarre large stone of marvelous workmanship, which is called the Pet-au-Diable. And at the Porte Baudet they sold many provisions....

XXVIII

OF THE GATES, AND FIRST OF ALL OF THE HIGH PART OF THE CITY[5]

The Porte [Saint-]Victor, outside of which is the Abbey of Saint-Victor, near the city; and at that point there is a very large fir-tree. The Porte Saint-Marcel, beyond which are the parish churches of Saint-Marcel, Saint-Médard, and Saint-Hippolyte.

[4] Jean de Beuil?

[5] The Left Bank.

Item: there is the collegiate church of Saint-Marcel and the retreat of the Cordeliers.

Item: there is a very large faubourg [Saint-Marcel], as if this was a separate town: workers from various trades lived there, especially butchers, dyers, tomb-workers, blade-workers, and others. The Porte Saint-Jacques, where there is a faubourg; there is the hospital of Saint-Jacques-du-Haut-Pas and the church of Notre-Dame-des-Champs. The Porte d'Enfer, which they now call the Porte Saint-Michel; beyond which is the Carthusian monastery. And there is the building called the wine-press of the Hôtel-Dieu, which extends from the said gate to the said Carthusian monastery. The Porte Saint-Germain: There are faubourgs where many butchers live; there is the abbey of Saint-Vincent, presently called the abbey of Saint-Germain-des-Prés, whose abbot exercises high, middle, and low justice. The Porte d'Orléans, next to which is the Nesle postern, beyond which is the ground called Pré-aux-Clercs.[6]

XXX

The Fifth Part in which Is Described the Excellence of the City in General

In Paris there were usually estimated more than 4,000 wine taverns, more than 80,000 beggars, more than 60,000 scribes.

Item: students and craftsmen without number.

Item: the flock of prelates and princes constantly frequenting Paris, the nobles, the deputies, the rich and divers marvels, solemnities, and happenings could in no way be

[6] The gates of the Right Bank are discussed in the following chapter (XXIX).

perfectly recounted. It was estimated that the gold, silver, and precious stones in the relics and plate of the churches of Paris was worth a great kingdom. They ate in Paris each week altogether 4,000 lambs, 240 steers, 500 calves, 200 salted and 400 unsalted hogs.

Item: each day they sold 700 casks of wine, of which the king has his quarter share, not including the wine of the students and others who pay no duties, like the lords and several others who receive it from their estates.

It was a signal event in Paris when Master Eustache de Pavilly, Master Jehan-Jarçon, Brother Jacques le Grand, the master of the Mathurins, and other doctors and clerics used to preach such excellent sermons, and the beautiful divine service that they celebrated then.

Item: when the kings of France, Navarre, and Sicily, a number of dukes, counts, prelates, and other notable lords constantly frequented here.

Item: when resided here Master Gilles des Champs, sovereign master of theology, Master Henri de Fontaines, astrologer, the Abbé Du Mont Saint-Michel, doctor of canon law, Bishop Du Puy, civil law, Master Thomas de Saint-Pierre, medicine, Master Gilles Sous-le-Four, surgery, and several excellent clerics of pleasing rhetoric and eloquence.

Item: when Master Laurent de Premierfait, the poet, recited; the German theologian, who played upon the hurdy-gurdy; Guillemin Dancel and Perrin de Sens, sovereign harpists; Cresceques, rebec player; Chynenudy, good blower of the bagpipe and flutes; Bacon, who played songs and tragedies on the hurdy-gurdy.

Item: Gobert, the sovereign scribe who composed *The Art of Writing and Cutting Quills;* and his disciples who by their good script were retained by princes, like the young Flamel by the duke of Berry, Sicart by King Richard [II] of

England, Guillemin by the grand master of Rhodes, Crespy by the duke of Orléans, Perrin by the Holy Roman Emperor Sigismund, and several others.

Item: several artificers, like Herman, who polished diamonds of various shapes; Willelm, the goldsmith; Andry, who worked in brass and copper, gilded and silvered; the potter who kept the nightingales who sang in winter; the three brothers, manuscript illuminators[7]; and others of ingenious trades.

Item: Flamel the elder, a scribe who gave so much alms and hospitality. He built several houses in which tradesmen lived downstairs, and the rent that they paid supported poor workmen upstairs.

Item: *la Belle Saunière, la Belle Bouchière, la Belle Charpentière,* and other ladies and damsels; *la Belle Herbière* and the one they exclaimed to be the most beautiful, and the one they simply called Belle.

Item: Damsel Christine de Pisan, who composed all sorts of knowledge and different treatises in Latin and French.

Item: the prince of loves,[8] who kept with him musicians and gallants, who knew how to compose and sing all sorts of songs, ballads, rondeaux, virelays, and other amorous ditties, and play melodiously upon instruments....

There used to come to Paris for diversion the emperor of Greece,[9] the emperor of Rome,[10] and other kings and princes from different parts of the world.

Item: at the coronation of the queen of France, Isabelle of Bavaria, when she first came to Paris,[11] there came with

[7] The Limbourg brothers.
[8] Probably an aristocrat-minstrel.
[9] Manuel II Paleologus; in 1400.
[10] Charles IV of Luxembourg; in 1378.
[11] In 1389.

her more than 120,000 persons on horseback, whom the queen paid.

Item: in the year 1418, in an epidemic, there died in the Hôtel-Dieu, near Notre-Dame, more than 30,000 persons, as it appeared in the Chambre des Comptes, where they delivered the shrouds for burial.

HERE ENDS THE DESCRIPTION OF THE CITY OF PARIS

III
THE VENETIAN AMBASSADOR'S SECRETARY

A DESCRIPTION OF PARIS IN 1577–1579, WRITTEN BY THE SECRETARY OF GIROLAMO LIPPOMANO, VENETIAN AMBASSADOR TO FRANCE[1]

INTRODUCTION

Beginning in the fifteenth century, the Venetian Republic, along with some other Italian states, established a network of resident ambassadors at the principal European courts. In addition to keeping the Venetian government informed about ongoing events, the ambassadors, upon their return, were required to make formal written reports to the Venetian

[1] Extracted and translated from "Viaggio del signor Girolamo Lippomano, ambasciator in Francia nell'anno 1577, scritto dal suo secretario," in Niccolò Tommaseo, ed., *Relations des ambassadeurs vénitiens sur les affaires de France au XVIe siècle* (Paris: Imprimerie Royale, 1838), 2:588–614 (with facing French translation, not always reliable). I thank Mr. Paolo de Ventura for help in making the present English translation. The original manuscript is in Paris, Bibliothèque Nationale de France, Département des manuscrits, ms. italien 1426, fols. 73–207.

Senate, which analyzed the personalities and politics at these courts and the economic and material conditions of the countries where they had served. These reports, which have survived, reveal the Venetian ambassadors as unusually acute, realistic observers of political, economic, and military affairs, and their accounts constitute prime sources for the modern historian ever since their rediscovery in the 1820s by the German historian Leopold von Ranke.

In addition to regular dispatches, ambassadors sometimes wrote a longer report about the political situation, and, upon completion of the mission, a "relation" (usually delivered orally to the doge and Senate) about the overall success of the mission, fleshed out with remarks of a wide-ranging nature about the foreign court and country, its geography, history, economy, customs, etc.

By the 1460s, certain Venetian ambassadors were provided with secretaries, who were separately appointed and accredited so that they could continue the ambassador's duties should he be incapacitated or recalled. It can be seen from this that secretaries had to be men of ability.

Girolamo Lippomano was the Venetian ambassador to the French court from 1577 to 1579. His anonymous secretary composed an extensive written account in two parts: the first contains a report on the events and personalities of these years; the second is a "relation," containing a physical description of France, the structure of its government, its customs and fashions, food, money, language, and other topics, including the description of Paris, which is presented here.

Lippomano and his secretary served during the unhappy reign of the French King Henry III (1574–89), which fell during the period of the Wars of Religion. Although the conflict and negotiations between French Catholics and Protestants are discussed by the secretary in the course of the "Viaggio," the struggle is not specifically touched upon in his pages on Paris; nevertheless, the writer's special concern with the military defenses of the city surely reflects the atmosphere in which he wrote, as do his observations about the practice of capital punishment, which conclude his account.

The secretary's "Description of Paris" reveals that he had absorbed the sober-eyed realism of the Venetian ambassadorial tradition. This is no eulogy of the city (Jean de Jandun), neither is it tinged in the least with nostalgia (Guillebert de Mets). Rather, Paris is seen through the eyes of an unsentimental viewer. Thus, in the course of the traditional description of Paris's architectural features, the secretary never omits an opportunity to point out a building's incompleteness, sometimes discussing the reasons for it. Or, for example, in mentioning the Cordeliers monastery, he remarks on the hardship and suffering of the novices.

After beginning with a discussion of the city's defenses, the "Description" proceeds to review the main public secular and religious structures, such as the Louvre, the Hôtel de Ville, Notre-Dame, etc. Architecture is of some interest to our writer, who provides details about the spiral staircase of the Tuileries Palace and features within the recently-created Tuileries Garden. The varied activities at the Palace are described, and particular attention is devoted to the many bridges linking the Île de la Cité with the Right and Left Banks.

This introductory, traditional section on the city's monuments is followed by comments on the economy, political personalities, royal finances, and police and judicial matters, all of which are recognized by our writer as integral parts of the urban reality. Here the secretary reveals a proto-modern awareness of the totality of urban factors more comprehensive than previously encountered.

The Parisian subsistence economy is of particular interest to this writer. There are notes on the basic provisions for the capital (food, wine, hay, wood, fodder, charcoal) and their transport; the high price of food and its remarkable abundance and elaborate preparation by people whom we recognize as incipient caterers and restaurateurs, found on all the main streets; the size of the population (commonly estimated, according to the secretary, at one million, including residents and foreigners, with at least thirty thousand university students); and the expensive house-rental market, which is closely analyzed. It is these pages that hint at the habits of mind of a modern urban economist.

The secretary directly comments on the two leading political personalities: the scheming queen-mother, Catherine de Médicis ("old and immersed by her ambition in the affairs of the kingdom") and her son, Henry III, of "slight reputation." The latter comment appears in a probing analysis towards the end of the "Description" of the ruinous state of the royal finances, in no small part due to the king's habit of enriching his favorites, as the secretary observes. He keenly recognizes that because Paris (along with Lyon) is the financial support of the monarchy — paying taxes, which some entire provinces withhold — the city was granted privileges and exemptions that attract immigrants from other parts of the kingdom, thus accounting for its large population.

Yet even during these difficult years, the secretary reports that Parisians continued to indulge in the pleasures of the table, and they had a passion for the game of tennis (he says there were more than 1800 courts!). But there is no further attempt to describe social habits. Paris emerges from these pages as a very crowded city, demographically and architecturally, the only open area being the horse market (on the site of the future Place des Vosges), itself in the process of being encroached upon by new houses. The Paris of boulevards and public squares has not yet come into being.

BIBLIOGRAPHY

On the Venetian ambassadors and their secretaries, see Garrett Mattingly, *Renaissance Diplomacy* (Boston: Houghton Mifflin, 1955); see also the introduction in Franco Gaeta, ed., *Relations des ambassadeurs vénitiens* (Paris: Klincksieck, 1969).

A Description of Paris in 1577–1579

Paris has twelve gates that are always open, except that of the Temple...and sometimes that of the Louvre, especially when the king is in Paris. But none of them can be called strong except that of Saint-Antoine, defended by the château of the Bastille, and that of the Louvre, protected by the royal château.

King Henry [II], either because he feared the schemes of Charles V or to better keep in check the Parisian people (which is good,[1] for they are permitted many things) was resolved to fortify the city, as one sees by the royal and superb construction that begins at the point of the Célestins and the Arsenal, and which runs almost to the Porte Saint-Martin. But because the cost, to speak the truth, was more than excessive, and necessity did not require more than that, the work was interrupted. If it were to be finished (which will never be done), this would be without doubt the most beautiful and the largest stronghold and fortress in the whole world. Nevertheless, it would face a major problem: it would need a numberless amount of soldiers to defend it. And even if it had proportionate forces, it could stand against the whole world only if provisions were not lacking. Besides, the number of soldiers that would be sought to guard the city would also be sufficent to guard

[1] Or "who are good" (referring to the Parisian people; the phrase is ambiguous): "ch'è buono perché se gli comportano molte cose."

the countryside: he who is master of the countryside is also master of provisions and many other commodities. The wall that is made of *pietra viva* [large stone blocks] is more than four *passa romane* in thickness; and the three bulwarks already completed are so large that each one would hold three thousand foot-soldiers and five hundred cavalrymen. So the work has been interrupted and will remain incomplete.

On the Right Bank of the Seine is the château of the Bastille, very strong though not very large, which now serves only as a prison for the princes or persons of distinction; and so there is no garrison. The palace or royal château [the Louvre], which is the residence of the court, is the beginning of a construction of majestic architecture; if it were ever finished, one could rightly say that it was one of the world's most beautiful edifices. King Henry [II] began it; but it is only one-fourth built. I have seen lodged at the Louvre the king and his brothers, three queens, two cardinals, two dukes with their wives, three princesses of the blood, many other favorites and ladies, and part of the council.

In the Faubourg Saint-Honoré there is that great start of construction of the Tuileries, a building of the queen-mother [Catherine de Médicis], with many statues, costly stones, so many orders of columns, and that spiral-stair, so wide and convenient, with steps not higher than four fingers, miraculously carried by a thin needle of marble. The stables are transformed into a magnificent palace; there is an apartment for tilting at the ring and practicing with weapons; and finally that beautiful garden where the trees and plants are distributed in an admirable order, where there are found not only labyrinths, *bosquets*, fountains, and rivulets, but also, distinctly reproduced, the seasons of the year and the signs of the zodiac, which is an unbelievable thing. But this building also will never be completed, for the queen-mother is old and immersed by her ambition in the affairs of the kingdom, so that, her lacking time as well as money, this construction will remain by necessity incomplete. It is intended to serve as a *maison de plaisance* for the princes, being so close to the royal palace that the king and the queens often go there on foot.

There is the very large church of Saint-Eustache, which, once finished, would be one of the most beautiful and largest of all Europe. I do not want to omit stating in this regard what I have heard from the mouth of the priest of this parish: that sometimes he has had 85,000 souls in his care, more than have many bishops of the main cities of Italy. There is also the abbey and church of Saint-Martin and the Temple, surrounded by high walls with turrets that give it the air of a château; and especially the Temple, which is a little smaller than the Arsenal of Venice. It is held at present by the natural brother of the king, grand-prior of the Order of Saint John of Jerusalem.

I do not speak about the houses of princes, like those of the dukes of Anjou, Bourbon, Lorraine, Guise, Montmorency, Damville (where we have been lodged for a long time, the ambassador [Lippomano] having spared nothing to have a residence suitable to his dignity); nor those of Brienne, Condé, Sens and many others, which does not seem necessary to me. Similarly, I shall not speak about the many public law-courts and trials that are in that part of the city. I shall mention simply the Hôtel de Ville, built in grand style, where the municipal magistrates, heads, and officers of the city assemble to present gifts and contributions to the king and where spectacles and banquets and similar proceedings are given to His Majesty in the name of the Parisian people. Here is the Mint, a building not elegant but rich in houses, offices, and shops, which give it the appearance of a large village. The Arsenal is not very big, in fact one can call it small considering the size of the city; they only work there on artillery pieces and on the making of gunpowder and cannon balls. A few years ago the gunpowder caught fire and caused such a great disaster that all the houses around Saint-Paul-des-Célestins were destroyed or shattered. But now the gunpowder is fabricated in another series of warehouses greatly separated one from another.

On the other side, the Left Bank of the river, is found the very large monastery of the Cordeliers, founded and built by Marguerite, wife of Saint Louis, which usually houses five hundred and sixty student-monks of that order, but truly under great hardship (as I have seen), for they suffer much in eating and dress. There is the abbey of Saint-Germain [-des-Prés], enclosed by moats and walls, and that of Saint-Victor, both of them very rich, and therefore belonging, the former to Cardinal de Bourbon, the latter to Cardinal de Guise. There is the great monastery of the Augustinians, the royal oratory. There is that great roof under which is held the Saint-Germain fair, which is as large as that of the Ascension in Venice. There is the university and the colleges, some of which lodge up to a thousand students.

On the Île [de la Cité], which lies in the middle of these two parts of the city, between the two branches of the river, is...the Sainte-Chapelle which, although a small edifice, is rich and officiated by a great number of priests. There is good music. This is one of the three holy chapels of France, all the more worthy than the other two, as the city of Paris is worthier than the others. It is situated moreover in the center of the city where there are so many holy relics; these are without doubt the most hallowed in all the world, except for Rome....

On this island is that famous and superb temple of Notre-Dame, entirely erected on piles of wood and indeed miraculous by its size and by the richness of the ornaments and the statues, with the most wondrous work on every side, inside and out, with two most beautiful towers — more than mere bell-towers — at the corners of the façade. Both are made with marvelous craft, of stone, adorned with capitals, figures, and other superb contrivances. At the top of these are the very large bells, one of which in particular is forty-five *palmi* in circumference. The nave of the church is slightly less wide than the Palazzo Ducale [Venice] above the courtyard. From this one can comprehend the remainder of this machine, disposed with such beautiful order and so correctly that it is a marvel, as well suits the cathedral of a city as large as Paris.

[On the Île de la Cité] is that palace, or public forum we might say, which the French call Le Palais. One usually sees there, morning and evening, an incredible number of judicial officials, litigants, errand-runners, merchants, and bankers. But that which is more delightful is in the great hall, where one sees the sculpted marble statues of all the kings and princes. And in the corridors, which are covered, there is an immense number of shops, as many as in the Merceria of Venice. One continually sees there a great number of cavaliers and ladies, even the king and the court itself; others come for amusement and pleasure, others to shop. And to speak the truth, one can say that the Palais is the lovers' go-between. It was formerly the usual royal residence.

The Pont Notre-Dame can be numbered among the most beautiful things in all of France. It is entirely of stone, so beautiful and wide that there are houses of stone as well on both sides, and sixty-eight attached shops of the same form and height; there is so much space in between that three vehicles can pass abreast. And it is so closed-in that he who had no experience of it would have judged it to be a street: this happened to me the first time I was in Paris. I was on this bridge and asked the way to get there; and since I was told I was there, I thought I was being made fun of. The Pont au Change...is also covered on both sides with houses and shops, more numerous than the Pont Notre-Dame, but they are almost all in roughcast and wood; the bridge itself rests on wooden piles, and therefore neither carts nor coaches are permitted to pass. This bridge is so-called because upon it and in the vicinity are found the shops of the goldsmiths and jewelers, in such numbers, I believe, as are found in three or four of the leading cities of Italy, not excluding Rome or Naples. The Pont des Moulins is of wood, built for the express use and accommodation of mills, all of wood; yet it is also loaded with small shops like that of the Rialto; and thus, for that reason, also, horses almost never pass there. The Petit-Pont...aligned with that of Notre-Dame, and that of Saint-Michel, aligned with the Pont au Change, are also both covered with large shops and houses in stone and roughcast. A bridge is being built now that will lead from the church of the Augustinians to the [Quai de l'École Saint-Germain]. It will be very beautiful, according to the design, and very convenient for those who live in the Faubourg Saint-Germain and in the neighborhood of the Louvre.

Such are the most remarkable and public of the buildings of Paris. There is no doubt that much of the city is occupied by racket-courts, the number of which rises to more than 1800, and it is calculated that a thousand *écus* daily are spent on tennis.... The French very much enjoy this game, which they play with so much elegance and comportment that it is a marvel.

Paris has in abundance everything that can be desired by human appetite. Not only merchandise from all parts of the world flows into it, but also foodstuffs from very distant lands, carried from Normandy, Auvergne, Burgundy, Champagne, and Picardy by the convenience of the river. And although the population is numberless,... nevertheless provisions are always in such plenty and abundance that they seem to rain down from heaven, albeit they are very expensive and high in price, for it is not by chance that the French do not spend as willingly for anything as for eating and for what they call good cheer. That is why we see so many butchers, provisioners, *rôtisseurs,* retailers, pastry-chefs, cabaret and tavern-keepers, so that it's a real confusion: there isn't a principal street that doesn't have all these conveniences. So that if you judge it more profitable to buy meat at the butcher and the animals at the market, you have the means of doing so at any turn, at any time, at any hour, and at any location in the city. If you want your food prepared, cooked, or raw, you have equally the *rôtisseurs* and the pastry-chefs, who in less than an hour arrange for you a dinner or a supper for ten, twenty, for a hundred and more persons, supplying all you want: the *rôtisseur,* the meat; the pastry-chef, the pâtés, the pies, the hors d'oeuvres and desserts; the cook, the aspics and the stews. And this art is so studied in this city that there are some tavern-keepers who feed you at their places according to the price one wants to pay, namely for one *teston,* for two, for one *écu,* for four, for ten, for twenty, if one can say so many, per person. But you must believe that they will give you manna, phoenix, or whatever is more excellent in this world, so that the princes and the king himself sometimes go there to eat....

The market for provisions is held twice a week: on Wednesdays and Saturdays there is poultry, hare, rabbit, goat kid, and young wild boar. Each time there is such a great quantity that one would think it would be sufficient for quite some time: nevertheless, what is supplied to one market never appears in the other, and in little more than two hours the square is always clear. Every Wednesday the wine market is also held; wine is brought, for the most part, via the river, from Orléans and Burgundy. The wines of the Île-de-France are not much valued. The tun [*tonneau*] is the largest of their measures, corresponding, I believe, to half a Venetian *botte*. The price, to speak the truth, is very variable from year to year; for in 1578 average quality wine was worth thirty francs a *muio,* or tun, as they say; in 1579, it was worth no more than nine or ten. Hay, wood, fodder, charcoal (all of which comes via the river) are sold, not at market, but immediately upon their arrival, even aboard the boats. They bring in the hay and straw bound in bundles, and they are sold by the bunch. Large-size wood is sold similarly by the bunch, like faggots and bundles; charcoal by measure, as is fodder and every type of grain. Meat and fish are sold according to appearance and in such great abundance that at no time did I see one or the other lacking.

Paris is not subject to being deprived of anything except wood and fodder, which are the two items that can only be brought by the river from time to time; so that each time that the river greatly rises (as in 1578) or freezes, the boats not being able to arrive, the city remains in a state of siege, especially in winter. There are almost always just under 100,000 pack and saddle horses; its outskirts barely produce hay for one month. But foodstuffs are not subjected to this difficulty, because in warm weather they are brought by the river without hindrance, and in winter by vehicles and horses. And yet there are so many people there to feed: according to common opinion there are continually in this city more than one million persons. The number is however impossible to know in a precise manner, not only because of the great multitude of foreigners who come and go every day, but because the inhabitants themselves (I mean the common people) change their dwellings every three months, so that one cannot keep an accurate register of them. But what is astonishing is that when the court comes and goes — for when it goes on long trips, it takes with it so many persons and shopkeepers that one could say an entire city was missing — one doesn't see any change in the city of Paris. Aside from a court so numerous, as one knows, and so abundant in princes, ladies, and courtiers, there is also the senate or Parlement, which occupies a large part of the most beautiful buildings of the city. It also has the university, which is rarely frequented by fewer than 30,000 students, that is to say more than have all the universities of Italy. The foreigners flock here in crowds, not only the provincials who come for their pleasure or to see the court, but also Germans, Flemings, Northerners [Scandinavians], Scotsmen, Englishmen, Italians, Spanish, Portuguese, and others. It is a confusion, less by diversity than by numbers. Hence there are so many public houses, rooms for rent, taverns, and cabarets in such density; so many provisioners and butchers; so many boats which sometimes completely cover the Seine; so many *rôtisseurs* and pastry-chefs that they could fill, without doubt, half the city or more; an amazing thing not only to see but also to hear about! Although food is in abundance, it is nevertheless higher in price and much more expensive, starting with meat, than in many parts of Europe.

This abundance of people and foreigners also very much maintains the high cost of house rentals. Usually the houses are rented completely furnished, by the day or by the month; for the concierges, who are actually the stewards of the houses and palaces, do not wish or are not able to arrange more time because of the uncertainty they always have that their masters will return to court. Then the tenants have to be driven from the house, if the masters wish it, especially if they are great lords. Thus Monsignor Salviati, the papal nuncio, was forced in our time to move three times in less than two months. It is quite true that there are some landlords who own their own houses and who rent them for as long as one wishes; but in conclusion there isn't one poor single furnished room that doesn't cost two or three *écus* per month.

Nevertheless, it is true that those who can find unfurnished houses are in a better situation; but it is necessary to take the trouble to buy the furniture. Then one is forced to lose in selling, because it is customary in this city to buy used things for one-third, even if in fresh condition. It is true that in less than two hours you can furnish a whole magnificent palace with any furnishings you want, cheap or expensive, kitchen plates, tapestries, linen, and in short everything needed for the furbishing of a household; there are also the auctions, which are held so often and in many locations around town....

[Paris] is not only the seat and ordinary residence, but also the true support and maintenance of the present French kings, through the great donations that they obtain from it. Indeed, it is impossible to write about or exactly calculate the income of the kingdom: payment of new taxes is refused, and in many provinces even the old ones are not discharged. It is supposed that the present king [Henry III] can usually expect about seven and a half million, including the income of the crown, the taxes, the tithes, and the rest; but because everything is very nearly assigned and pledged, the present king extracts with great difficulty a million and a half. That cannot suffice for the ordinary expenses and for the large gifts that His Majesty continually bestows, to his ruin and slight reputation. I shall cite as an example that the king not only dismembers the existing revenues in order to enrich his favorites, but that he also gives them those that come to the crown through war, confiscations, or in other ways. So that, because of bad management of the finances and the continual plunder of money by the officials and ministers, everything is in disarray. The ambassadors are not paid, the court is badly off, and the troops receive neither pay nor conveniences, unless they rob or murder poor village folk.

Thus the city of Paris alone and the stronghold of Lyon are those, one can say, that support the French kings and come to their aid in their most urgent need, for there are many provinces (as stated above) from which they don't even get a sou; and in those where collections are made, everything disappears in pensions and in repayments of old debts. That is why Paris enjoys privileges and exemptions that the other cities of the kingdom do not have and that attract there the great concourse of inhabitants who fill it entirely.

On the squares themselves one sees small shops of wood built by poor people who do the humblest jobs to survive. So that there is no part of the city that can be called vacant except the horse market, where one sees every Saturday a thousand or two thousand horses for sale, which looks like a whole military cavalry. But even there, in a few years, everything will be covered with houses; indeed, they are already and continuously building.

The courthouses are also located in different parts of the city, in smaller districts: close by are also the prisons, without number. In each of the main districts there is a small loggia where some officials have to stay, because sergeants are required, who are like infantrymen and commanders among us. But those who have care of the management of justice, and who make the rounds every night to seize delinquents, are called the watch [*le guet*]; their head is the knight of the watch. Each parish has a head or commissioner, as they are called, who commands a certain number of men obligated to keep a horse and to serve, even in open country if necessary. Indeed, during the night many of these come riding through the city with such a clamor, that they give evil-doers the signal and the time to save themselves.

The prisons (as I have said) are numerous, and all are almost always full. One sees nevertheless almost every day in one part of the city or in another the execution of people, mostly through hanging. And more than that, those who are sentenced *in absentia,* since they can't be actually held, are made to die in effigy, namely by affixing their image to the gallows. In such cases the expense is the same, the same ceremony is enacted, as if the actual body of the criminal were there. The mounted watch proceeds as guard, the image is carried on a wagon, and is even accompanied by a priest: which is something rather barbarous.

IV
GIOVANNI PAOLO MARANA

AN ITALIAN LETTER WRITTEN BY A SICILIAN CONTAINING A PLEASANT CRITIQUE OF PARIS[1]

1692

INTRODUCTION

Giovanni Paolo Marana was born in or near Genoa about 1643, perhaps of a noble family. His early education is undocumented; he certainly learned Latin, but was probably and essentially an autodidact. In 1670 he was involved in a plot to deliver Genoa into the hands of the duke of Savoy, and as a result of the failure of the coup, Marana was

[1] First published as "Traduction d'une lettre italienne écrite par un Sicilien à un de ses amis, contenant une critique agréable de Paris," in [Charles Cotolendi], *Saint Evremoniana, ou Dialogues des nouveaux dieux* (Paris: M. Brunet, 1700), pp. 374–425. The translation given below follows this publication, reproducing its paragraph divisions. There is a modern annotated edition, with some errors and omissions in Marana's text: (Jean-Paul) Marana, *Lettre d'un Sicilien à un de ses amis*, ed. Valentin Dufour (Paris: A. Quantin, 1883) (Collection des anciennes descriptions de la France, vol. 9). The anonymous translation may be due to François Pidou de Saint-Olon; the original Italian text is lost.

imprisoned (1670–74). The years following his release saw him in Genoa, Monaco, and Lyon, where, in 1682, he published a history of the conspiracy. In the same year he moved to Paris where, between 1684 and 1686, there appeared the first edition of his most important work, *L'espion du Grand Seigneur,* published anonymously and soon translated into English and continued by an unknown collaborator as *Letters Writ by a Turkish Spy* — an important source for Montesquieu's *Lettres persanes* (1721). (The many references to the Orient and Islam in the "Letter" can be seen as a link to *L'espion.)* An admirer of Louis XIV, Marana in 1688 published *Les événements les plus considérables du règne de Louis le Grand.* He died in Paris in 1693.

The "Letter Written by a Sicilian" appeared in 1700 in a volume of writings, most of which are attributed to Charles Cotolendi, the presumed translator of Marana's Italian text that became *L'espion du Grand Seigneur.* The "Letter" was republished several times as an anonymous work, but in 1883 Dufour, in his annotated edition, assigned it to Marana. Subsequent scholarship has generally agreed with this attribution (rejecting Saint-Evremond or Cotolendi as the author), although not without some hesitation. If it is indeed by Marana, then the "Letter" dates from the very end of his life.

The "Letter" was not written by a Sicilian (Marana was Genoese), and its considerable length suggests that it was composed as a literary essay, not as an actual epistle to an actual friend. But these fictive elements should not deter us from accepting the "Letter" as a veracious (albeit very personal) portrayal of Paris in 1692 as penned by a cultivated Italian (the "Letter" is studded with classical references) who had lived in the city for a decade (as he states at the very beginning, thus corresponding to Marana's known arrival in 1682).

The epistolary form — new in the history of city descriptions, and one that was to flower in the following century, as demonstrated by our next writer — allowed Marana to write in a familiar and witty manner. The author avoids any systematic organization of his material; he glides easily, even randomly, from topic to topic, sometimes circling back to a subject discussed a few pages before. As a result, the reader has the impression of listening to a loquacious, spontaneous, and entertaining raconteur and keen observer of the Parisian scene (he even comments on the changeable weather). The result is a vivid evocation of the texture of Parisian life in the latter part of the Sun King's reign.

Marana's Paris of 1692 was a quite different place from the late sixteenth-century capital that Lippomano's secretary described. By 1692 Paris was a much larger and even more populous city, embellished with new public squares and magnificent modern buildings in classical styles, with an opera house and theaters. There was a much greater presence of foreign visitors than in Lippomano's day, testimony to the intellectual and cultural prestige that the city enjoyed and its close proximity to the newest wonder of the modern world, Louis XIV's palace and gardens at Versailles. Although the latter was the seat of the court and government (officially since 1682), there was a constant presence of aristocrats, courtiers, and officials in Paris throughout the reign. Paris, to Marana, was the equivalent of France itself, and so he frequently speaks of Frenchmen when he is ostensibly describing only the Parisians. This generalizing habit reflects the reality of Parisian dominance in French cultural life that has persisted down to our own day.

Above all, the atmosphere of Paris was peaceful, for Louis XIV's wars were fought on or beyond France's frontiers, far from the city, whose defensive ramparts had been converted into spacious boulevards. The prayer for peace at the conclusion of the "Letter" is a reference to the War of the Grand Alliance, then raging on several fronts, but not on French soil. Paris, as Marana notes, was now the modern Babylon, a city of infinite pleasures (so it has remained), but the "Letter" also bears witness to the great expansion in size and population by its references to the crowding, tumult, and noise.

Marana transports us, more vividly than any previous writer, into the quotidian experience of Old Paris. We hear the cries of roosters at daybreak, the perpetual motion and clamor of men, horses, and coaches with their gruff drivers with cracking whips, the tolling of numerous church bells, the cries of hawkers in the streets. There are sketches of the urban scene: the greats of the town rumbling by in their coaches, their servants mounted at the rear, noble ladies in churches and gardens, trailing gowns of gold and silk, the *beau monde* in the Tuileries Garden; but we also glimpse the overcrowded houses, the blind beggars, the thieves, the mud and filth, and much more: the modern city, with its contrasts and miseries, is coming into being.

Some of the features observed by Marana were reported by our earlier writers, testimony to continuities in Parisian life: shops with luxury merchandise (Jean de Jandun); the numerous taverns, abundance of food, and eating at all hours; the nightwatch; the local police sergeant or commissioner; and the popularity of tennis (all reported by the Venetian secretary). But Marana also mentions two urban features that we have not previously encountered: street-lighting (instituted from 1667 on, although occasionally used in the late sixteenth century) and, especially, horse-drawn coaches and carriages, the new form of rapid transportation, invented in the sixteenth century and popularized in the seventeenth.

But the "Letter" is only minimally concerned with the physical appearance of the metropolis. There is almost no mention or description of architecture (not even Notre-Dame or the Louvre!) except for two features — the Pont-Neuf and the Tuileries Garden — and these are of interest to Marana mainly because they serve as backdrops or frames for human activity. Specific works of art are not mentioned except for the equestrian statue of Henry IV on the Pont-Neuf, praised for the sculptor's skill in conveying the king's martial ardor. Yet Marana makes an important observation about Parisian domestic architecture when he notes that although the exteriors of houses are plain, the interiors are richly furnished, with a preference for tapestries over sculpture (the latter popular in Italy).

Marana, however, is primarily an observer of social behavior, and he is keenly aware (as were all his contemporaries) of gender and class distinctions. He has much to say about Parisian women — their power, freedom, frequently good education, and sex-lives — and he also gives us some scathing pages on lawyers (and endless law-suits), physicians, servants, thieves, and other denizens, who do not escape his satirical pen. Portraits of Parisian types and social habits: that is what Marana offers as central to a description of a city.

We must ask, however, whether Marana's observations on the city, its types, social classes, and human conduct are based solely upon actual experience, or whether they are flavored, to some extent, by his reading. Consider, for example, these lines from Nicolas Boileau's sixth Satire, published in 1666:

> For scarcely shall the roosters, beginning their crowing,
> Have struck the neighborhood with their sharp cries,
> Than a horrible metal-worker, whom Heaven in its wrath
> Has placed, for my sins, too close to my place,

With a cursed iron, which he prepares with great noise,
With a hundred hammer blows is going to split my head.
I already hear everywhere the running of the carts,
The masons working, the shops opening:
While in the air a thousand bells set in movement
Make the clouds resound with a funereal concert,
And, mingling with the sound of the hail and the wind,
Make the living die to honor the dead.

(ll. 15–26)

Although more desperate in tone, these lines recall some of Marana's opening descriptions of the city. His mordant pages devoted to lawyers and physicians stem from old satirical traditions and, with reference to the latter, recall Molière (*Le malade imaginaire; Monsieur de Pourceaugnac*). And his penchant to moralize at every turn (as when, after mentioning the high price of imported oranges and lemons, he writes: "Such is human inclination, which only finds good in what is expensive") suggests the influence of contemporary French moralists, particularly Jean de La Bruyère, whose *Caractères* first appeared in 1688. Marana, for example, returns several times to the themes of fickleness and changing fashion, which he sees at the core of Parisian (and French) character ("It is *fashion* that is the real demon that always torments this nation"), and these are topics that La Bruyère treats in a number of passages in his book, although, unlike Marana, he views them as universal human weaknesses. In this connection, we may note Marana's observation that "Moral philosophy is mainly to the taste of the French; they write about it with much refinement."

The possibility of such influences upon Marana calls for special study (he is still a comparatively neglected figure), but even if they can be conclusively demonstrated, they would not necessarily detract from the authenticity of his

Parisian impressions. For it may be asked, what observer of an urban scene is totally unaffected by what he or she has previously read and heard about a given city and its inhabitants? This is an open question that can be asked of every writer in this anthology.

A final word should be said about Marana's pose as a Sicilian (we remember that he was really Genoese). This was an outgrowth of the strategy he had devised for *L'espion du Grand Seigneur (Letters Writ by a Turkish Spy)*. In that work, a Turk named Mahmut, sent to spy on the French by the Ottoman sultan, lives in Paris for decades and writes back to Turkish ministers, his family, and friends about his experiences in the French capital. This may have been the first use of the literary device of the foreign observer, which gave Marana license to comment very freely on Parisian culture as if he were a visitor from an exotic land, with a radically different outlook on Western institutions and customs. It is a distancing technique in the service of criticism and satire, later used in the eighteenth century by Montesquieu (*Lettres persanes*, 1721), the Marquis d'Argens (*Lettres juives*, 1738; *Lettres chinoises*, 1739–40; *Lettres cabalistiques*, 1741), Oliver Goldsmith (*The Citizen of the World*, 1762), and others. In the same way, Marana's Sicilian mask in the "Letter" placed him at a farther remove from Paris than his real Genoese identity, not merely geographically, but culturally as well. The contemporary French view of Sicily is conveyed by Molière's one-act farce, *Le Sicilien ou l'Amour Peintre* (1667). Here, Sicily is presented as a land of masters and their exotic slaves, a contrast to France. Marana's discussion of the frequency of kissing among the French reminds us of these lines from *Le Sicilien*, in which the Sicilian lord, Dom Pèdre, introduces Adraste (a Frenchman posing as a painter) to his Greek slave, the beautiful Isidore, whom Adraste is engaged to paint:

Dom Pèdre: [speaking to Isidore] Here is a gentleman whom Damon [a French painter] sends us, who is willing to take the trouble to paint you. (Adraste kisses Isidore upon greeting her, and Dom Pèdre says:) Stop! French seigneur, this sort of greeting is not customary in this land.

Adraste: It's the French way.

Dom Pèdre: The French way is good for your women; but, for ours, it is a bit too familiar. Scene XII

Molière, although his sympathies are clearly with Adraste, sketches a cultural contrast. Similarly for Marana, the observations of a Sicilian in Paris, rather than of a Genoese, were a means of providing a wider and more pungent perspective on Parisian life.

BIBLIOGRAPHY

See the Introduction by Valentin Dufour to the 1883 edition cited above. See also Gian Carlo Roscioni, *Sulle tracce dell "Esploratore turco"* (Milan: Rizzoli, 1992) (the "Letter" is discussed on pp. 228ff.); Yvonne Bellenger, "La description de Paris dans la *Lettre d'un Sicilien,* datée de 1692," in *La découverte de la France au XVIIe siècle,* Neuvième colloque de Marseille organisé par le Centre Méridional de Rencontres sur le XVIIe siècle, 25-28 janvier 1979 (Colloques internationaux du C.N.R.S., no. 590) (Paris: C.N.R.S., 1980) pp. 119-32. Selections from Marana's *magnum opus* are available as *Letters Writ by a Turkish Spy,* ed. Arthur J. Weitzman (New York: Temple University Publications/Columbia University Press, 1970), with an important introduction by the editor.

A Pleasant Critique of Paris

My Friend,

It is almost ten years since I have been in Paris and I still don't know the city well. Don't think that the pleasures, which are infinite in this great Babylon, prevent me from improving myself; on the contrary, these are the same pleasures that have given me an extreme desire to get to know it....

You who know my manner of living and my inclinations, you can imagine for yourself how I live here. Ordinarily I rise in the morning as soon as the sun appears; but that great luminary does not allow itself to be seen often: that results in its being here in greater veneration than are the rulers of China in their empire, since it passes half the year as if it were invisible.

I am always awakened very early in the morning; the cries of the roosters open my eyes, and the noise of men and horses brings me fully out of sleep. My main pleasure is to read when I am not writing, or to read and write at the same time. Having finished the morning's study, which is the movement of the mind, I begin the movement of the body, and I find no greater diversion than strolling. When the weather is fine, I walk in beautiful and long avenues in the shade of trees; we call that "promenading," an exercise that the Turks cannot bear and which appears ridiculous to the Asiatics; every day then I do several miles without traveling. For that purpose, the king [Louis XIV] maintains for idlers the most beautiful garden in Europe [the Tuileries Garden].

Concerning Paris, I don't know where to begin to paint for you a picture of a city whose inhabitants are lodged even on the bridges of the river and on the roofs of houses, and where the women, who produce only duellists, have more authority than the men. This great city is the seat of tumult, and since you want a sort of description of it, I shall begin with the perpetual movement that reigns here day and night.

When the tutor of Nero [Seneca] wrote on the tranquillity of life, I believe that he chose the subject from the hired carriages of his time, in contrasting repose to the continual noise that they made in Rome. There are here a great number of them, which are badly maintained and covered with mud and which are made only to kill the living. The horses who pull them eat while walking, like those who led Seneca to the countryside — to such a degree are they thin and emaciated. The coachmen are so brutal, their voices are so hoarse and dreadful, and the continual cracking of their whips increases the noise in so horrible a manner that it seems that all the Furies are in movement to make of Paris a hell. This cruel vehicle is paid for by the hour, a custom invented to abridge the days in an age when life is so short.

Moreover, the great number of large bells suspended at the tops of a huge number of towers removes tranquillity from the highest region of the air with their mournful reverberations in order to call the living to prayers and to grant repose to the dead; thus do the ears pay dearly for the innocent pleasures that all the other bodily members can procure.

If formerly an emperor had the whimsy to judge the extent of Rome by weighing all the spiders' webs that he had collected around the entire circumference of that great city, the extent of Paris could be measured with greater reason by the extreme quantity of footmen, horses, dogs, litigants, and thieves found there; all these people constitute a third of the population. Add to this the yelling and the cries of all those who go about the streets selling herbs, dairy products, fruit, rags, gravel, brooms, fish, water, and a thousand other necessities of life, and I don't believe that there is anyone in the world born deaf who is so much his own enemy that he might want at this price to receive hearing to listen to such a diabolical uproar.

Deprivation of sight is very honored here; I have never seen such a large number of blind people. They go through all the city without guides and walk in groups amidst an infinite number of carts, carriages, and horses with the same sureness as if they had eyes in their feet. They live together in a large building called the Hospital of the Quinze-Vingts, where they are fed by the alms of the people, in commemoration of three hundred French gentlemen whose eyes were put out in bygone times by a sultan of Egypt. They sing psalms in that hospital; they marry each other, produce children, and make merry. They especially do not fail to torment the faithful in all the churches, from whom they ask alms with a copper cup in one hand and a stick in the other, and in such a loud voice as if the Christians were those same statues from which formerly the Cynic of Athens [Diogenes] asked for help in order to acquire patience.

The houses here seem built by philosophers rather than by architects, to such a degree are they plain on the exterior; but the interiors are well embellished. However, they contain nothing extraordinary except the magnificence of the tapestries that cover the walls, it not being customary in France to decorate the latter with sculpture.

The great are distinguished by not wanting to do anything to serve others and by a great number of two-legged beasts and animals who always follow them when they are drawn along in their coaches. The horses precede the footmen, it being the fashion to place the latter upon the rear of the coach, in crews, with straight legs like the Colossus of Rhodes and clasped together in an indecent posture, as if they were entering in triumph into the city of Pentapolis.

It is no exaggeration to say that all Paris is a great hostelry; everywhere are seen cabarets and inn-keepers, taverns and tavern-keepers. The kitchens exude smoke at all hours because one eats at all hours; to take lunch and eat all day long are the same thing in France. The French don't like the spices of the Levant, not that they scorn these precious seasonings, but because they are the delicacies of the Spanish and the Italians, they do not wish to imitate other nations, even in good things.

They do nothing with stinginess; their tables are always abundant; they never eat alone; they love to take small but frequent sips; and they never drink without inviting their guests to do the same. The lower class only gets drunk on holidays when there is no work, but it labors on working days with assiduity. There are no people in the world who are more industrious and gain less, because they spend all on their stomachs and dress, and yet they are always content.

Luxury is here in such excess that, to enrich three hundred deserted cities, it would suffice to plunder Paris. One sees flourishing here a great number of shops in which are only sold things that one doesn't need; judge by the numbers of others where one buys necessities.

The river called the Seine passes through the middle of the city; it brings to it everything necessary to nourish a million persons. Its waters are tranquil and beneficial; men and animals drink it; but it is always sold, whether it is clear or muddy. What I find unjust is that a bucket of water costs the same whether the river is high or low.

The necessities of life are seen in abundance and in all parts of the city. Themistocles would have found in each street of Paris the three cities that the king of Persia gave him: one for bread and the two others for wine and clothing. Everything is obtained here in the same place, for necessity and for pleasure, pleasure being as sought after as what is needed: so much do vain and useless things have power over people.

Though it may not be raining, one can't help often walking in mud; they throw all the filth in the street, but the vigilance of the magistrates isn't sufficient to have them cleaned; nevertheless the ladies no longer go about on mules. Formerly the men couldn't walk in Paris except in ankle boots; this caused a Spaniard to ask, seeing them in this gear the day of his arrival, if the entire town was leaving in haste.

One sees several bridges over the river, some of wood and some of stone; there are some on which have been built a great many pleasant houses and several shops filled with precious merchandise. But the Pont-Neuf seems more worthy of the city than of the river; it is supported by twelve great arches of massive stones; it is wide and majestic; and it is mainly there where are found night and day the coaches, the horses, the carts, and the people, in perpetual motion. One sees there, in the middle, the equestrian statue of Henry the Great [Henry IV], elevated on a magnificent pedestal, majestic and worthy of such a great king. It seems that the bronze, although cold, still breathes the martial ardor of that warrior-prince, so vividly has the artisan represented him.

The women here love little dogs with extreme passion, and they caress them with so great a tenderness as if they were descended from the dog that followed Tobias. The women are the most beautiful and the most ugly ornament of the city, because the beautiful ones are rare. But they surpass in charm and vivacity all the women of the world, with the result that they have the ability to persuade, to win everything for themselves, and never to lose at anything. They also have the privilege of giving orders to their husbands and of obeying no one. The freedom of this sex is here greater than that enjoyed by the Arabs in the countryside, who never sleep during the night in the place where they had arisen in the morning. They are both subtle and eloquent; they sell merchandise in public in the shops and squares and yield to men neither in the art of calculating nor in that of quibbling and selling dearly even things that are left over.

Those who pride themselves in being learned give quarter to no one, and when they hold in their heads the maxims of Aminta and Corisque, there is no Xenocrates severe enough not to be persuaded. Some of them are going to Parnassus in the company of poets, and since the ignorance of even useless things is condemned here, almost all the women boast of having had masters to teach them and of having stepped forth from some school. Thus there are some who write and who compose books; the wisest bear children and the most pious console the afflicted; the most moderate eat as many times daily as the Mohammedans pray, it being the custom of the land to salute the rising sun with bread in one's hand.

All of them dress with much propriety; they are seen at all hours; they love the conversation of merry people; they go about town as it pleases them; the doors of their houses are always open to those who have entered only once. They hate no one, except when they are mocked concerning those things that Lamia made known to King Demetrius that were injurious to their sex, that is to say when a man boasts about what he did not do and when he doesn't keep his word. They often change the fashion of their clothes, as they often change their faces.

There are some who, when leaving their houses, neglect to close the door in defiance of thieves, because they carry with them their entire inheritance. The noblest drag behind them a long train of gold or silk, with which they sweep the churches and the gardens. They all have the privilege of going masked at all times, to hide or reveal themselves when it pleases them, and with a mask of black velvet they sometimes enter the churches as at a ball or the theater, unknown to God and their husbands. The most beautiful give orders to men as if they were queens, to their husbands as if they were any man, and to their lovers as if they were slaves. They don't know what it is to suckle their children, to be shut up within their houses, to weave Penelope's cloth, making fun of Hercules who turns the spindle. And in living with such freedom, they boast of producing generals and men of letters, in which this land abounds, there being found here more soldiers and savants than superstitious people and astrologers in the Indies and in Asia.

They give and receive love easily, but do not love for a long time nor sufficiently. Marriages, which formerly were for life, at this moment are only for a time; that results in voluntary divorce being easily found in the most discreet houses, after which the husband lives quietly in the provinces and the wife enjoys herself in Paris.

One almost never sees here jealous persons, rarely a man who considers himself wretched because of his wife's infidelity, and very rarely a daughter who sacrifices to Diana. The kiss, which in Turkey, Italy, and Spain is the beginning of adultery, is here only a simple civility, and if that noble Persian, who made so many mysterious voyages to kiss the handsome Cyrus three times, found himself in Paris, he wouldn't have placed a high value on the pleasure that he had. There are no visits where kisses are not exchanged; but the former are of the quality of coins that are valued as one wishes, and since the kiss is a piece of merchandise that costs nothing, that is never used up and always abounds, no one is miserly in giving them and few are eager to take some.

Fickleness is the fifth element of the French; they are lovers of novelties, and they do all they can not to keep a friend too long. They adapt at the same time to cold and heat; they invent every day new fashions to dress in; and, always growing bored with living in their country, one sees them going sometimes to Asia and sometimes to Africa, few to Spain, more to Italy, and to a great number of different lands, for the sole purpose of changing their location and amusing themselves. Those who cannot travel treat their houses like their clothes: they frequently change dwelling, for fear, they say, of growing old in the same place.

The tailors have more trouble inventing than sewing, and when clothes last more than the life of a flower, they seem worn out. From that is born a race of old-clothes dealers, base people, descended from ancient Israel; their profession is to buy and sell old rags and used clothes, and they live splendidly by despoiling some and dressing others — a rather singular advantage in a very populous city, where those who grow tired of wearing the same clothes for a long time change them at a moderate loss, and where the others who lack some have the means to dress themselves at small expense. Finally, what is more unbelievable, is that if, in a single day, a hundred thousand litigants emerge naked from the hands of attorneys, there are in this city enough shirts and clothes to cover their nakedness.

The language of the French is a noble mixture of Latin, Italian, and Spanish; it is pleasing only to him who has good hearing. They eat half their words; they don't write as they speak, and they take pleasure in speaking so as not to be understood, so rapid and hasty is their manner of pronunciation, although at present their language is refined and gracious.

Since they grow bored with talking about present matters, they discourse always about the future, rarely about the past, and never about antiquity; they believe that it is a vice of the Spanish to go and disinter distant centuries, and they seek out only recent books, young horses, and friends born on the same day.

One knows a true Frenchman by four things: when the clock strikes, when he questions someone, when he makes a promise, and when he talks about his love-affairs. Scarcely has the clock begun to strike when he asks what time it is; he wishes that his friend answer him before being questioned; he only does what he hasn't promised; and as for his love affairs, he takes more pleasure in proclaiming the favors of his mistress than in receiving them.

If the change in weather forces the French to dress in wool in the morning and in silk after dinner, the fickleness of their spirit also obliges them to fashion for themselves new manners of living and of attire.

Luxury and good living would be two blessings here rather than two evils, if there were only the rich who lived splendidly; but jealousy passes them on to others, to whom they become ruinous. Thus it seems that Paris continually approaches her end, if it is true, as an ancient says, that "excessive spending is the clear sign of a dying city." But since at present the footmen and the coachmen begin to wear scarlet and feathers, and that gold and silver have become commonplaces even on their clothing, there is the likelihood that we are going to see the end of excessive luxury, since there is nothing that makes us so despise the gilded clothes of noble persons as seeing them on the bodies of the lowest people in the world.

Only the king is obeyed, and there isn't a great lord who dares to threaten the most insignificant. When you have rendered to the master what is due him, then you can live in Greek fashion; one isn't obliged in the street to doff one's hat before whomever, unless it is before God, when the Crucifix is brought to the sick. The dregs of the people enjoy the same privilege; they do not let anyone pass ahead of them by deference; they do not tolerate the slightest insult, and they gain more respect than the honest people, unaware of what is occurring in the republics, where a thousand masters give orders to an infinite number of slaves.

There isn't a haughtier or more impudent people; they themselves have earned the reputation of not doing anything in the evening that they had promised in the morning. They say that they are the only people in the world who have the privilege of breaking their word without fear of doing anything against honesty, and that because they believe themselves to be the only ones in the world who know how to enjoy true liberty.

Rooms are very expensive here; a small bedroom is worth more than ten houses in Muscovy. Mine, where Plato would not want to sleep and where even Diogenes would find nothing superfluous, forces me to an expense that ten Cynics could not afford. Yet all my furnishings consist only of a mediocre tapestry that covers four thin walls, a bed, a table, a few chairs, a mirror, and a portrait of the king.

Bad things are more expensive than good ones; figs are of this number: more are sold than melons in Spain. Assuredly Eve would not have disobeyed God in the Armenian paradise if the forbidden fruit had been one of these figs; but in exchange the pears are excellent.

Oranges and lemons hold the first rank among things that are sold for a high price, because they come from Italy and Portugal and are more esteemed than the other fruits. Such is human inclination, which only finds good in what is expensive.

Wine costs a moderate price at the city gates, but as soon as it is brought within, it changes into potable gold; a small measure is worth more in Paris than a cask in the countryside. The wealthy people find this liquid more expensive than the others, who buy it by counted measures in the taverns. The tavern-keepers are in such great numbers that they would populate a large city; almost all of them are saints by the power that they have of increasing this liquid by changing water into wine, that is to say in rendering Bacchus adulterated.

If you ever come to Paris, beware of stepping into the shops where they sell useless things. As soon as the merchant has described his stock to you with several rapid words, he flatters you and by degrees invites you with many bows to buy something, and in the end he talks so much that he annoys you and makes you dizzy. When you enter his shop, he begins by showing you everything you don't want, followed by showing you what you ask for, and then he speaks and acts so nicely that you spend all your money in taking the goods that he gives you for more than they are worth.

This is how they are recompensed for their civility and the continual pains they take in uselessly showing, a hundred times a day, their merchandise to sight-seers who want to see all without buying anything. If indeed the useless things cost more than the others, I find that the Roman censor was correct in saying that "that which costs an obol is very expensive when it isn't necessary."

Today it has rained in the morning, fine weather at noon, then it snowed, and all of a sudden a storm arose with rain that lasted two hours; at last the air appeared quiet and the sun showed itself, finishing the day pleasantly. Such is the Parisian climate: the evening warmth succeeds the morning cold. The elements here are in perpetual movement and the seasons are almost always in disorder. The sky is never in repose and its influences are always unequal; there is no persistence except in bad things, especially in winter, which lasts eight months here with all the rigors of that season, which come one after the other: rain, snow, hail, frost, fog, and dark weather, which hides the sun for months at a time. It is therefore not a great surprise if the French, accommodating themselves to the inconstancy of their climate, are so filled with fickleness, and if the ladies carry at the same time a muff in one hand and a fan in the other.

During Lent the people hurry in the morning to the sermon with great devotion, and after dinner to the theater with the same alacrity. There are here three theaters, which are continually open to delight those who love these kinds of pleasures: in one they present shows with music, and the two others are filled, one by the French comedians and the other by the Italian comedians. Each company vies with the other to attract spectators, but the crowd is found in the theater where one laughs more; that is why the Italian comedians profit more than the French comedians from popular simplicity.

The lawyers, the charlatans, the gamblers, and the footmen form one of the finest ornaments of Paris: the first teach us never to go to court for fear that they will consume our wealth by their chicanery; the second show us the way to live soberly in order not to fall into their hands and be killed by their remedies; the gamblers excite our vigilance to preserve our wealth; and the footmen have found the secret of making us appreciate the pleasure of serving ourselves, "in order not to have," as the Lord says, "enemies in our house."[1] The footmen say among themselves that the German servants are chums with their employers, that the English servants are slaves, the Italians respectful, the Spanish submissive, but that they, the French servants, are the only ones who give orders to their masters. Their insolence is extreme, and the king has forbidden them, under grave penalties, to carry batons, with which they caused recent disorders every day, especially since there are more than a hundred thousand capable of all sorts of outbursts.

The place where the Parlement meets [the Palais] forms a city in the midst of the city itself. This place is only frequented by those who are defending their wealth or who wish to have that of others; Diogenes, with his lantern, would not find there two friends or a contented man.

[1] An echo of Micah 7.6 and Matthew 10.36.

The attorneys, who are in herds in all the towns of France, are found here in the thousands; they are a type of men chosen to remove the fat from those who are too fat and to prevent the thin from growing fat. It seems that the princes only put up with them in order to maintain a sort of civil war among their subjects, persuaded that, if they do not spend their lives demanding at law what belongs to them and usurping what doesn't belong to them, the princes' authority would be in danger by their subjects' intrigues and agitation. When I enter the Grand'Salle, I see an infinite number of excited individuals, half of whom torment the other half with stubborn disputes several years old, supported by the diabolical inventions of the practitioners. Their robes are long and black, to show how they are baneful to everyone; they wear on their heads a cap with four horns, after the fashion of priests, and in this costume they lead their parties as so many victims upon the altar of Justinian.

Their weapons are the language, the pen, and the purse: with the first two they defend and ruin their clients, and with the purse they strip them. They only finish the cases when the parties have no more money to continue them, and when they are judged, the litigants are left only with a mass of scribbled papers, filled with a type of magical wording that no one can understand. It is upon this battlefield where father and child, husband and wife, master and servant do combat with one another with blows of the pen, with threats, injuries, and calumnies, and where one sees actual extortion, sums denied, thefts by tutors, and the tears of widows and orphans.

When, at the end of many years, someone wins his suit, his victory reduces him to begging. This exercise in litigation has something bizarre about it: two adversaries solicit the same judge night and day, one in order to keep his shirt on his back and the other in order to go naked, experience showing only too often that he who wins his case has hardly enough to dress himself in, and the one who loses hasn't anything with which to cover himself.

Books are in the library of a famous lawyer like the fish that one sees in the sea, where one group eats the other. A million dead authors are arranged in battle, one against the other, in order to maintain sedition in all the families of the living, to such a degree are the opinions of these doctors, interpreters of the law, in opposition, doubtful, uncertain, and variable. It is thus that the laws of Justinian and of all the other princes are corrupted, violated, or confounded by these ignorant or malicious interpreters who do not know the truth of the law or who take pleasure in finding an unknown meaning, caring little that their subtle interpretation may become the source of an infinite number of bad disputes. The Spanish proverb seems very true to me, that "he who begins a lawsuit plants a palmtree," a tree that never bears its fruit to him who plants it. The Mohammedans are much more fortunate: their batons settle more lawsuits in two days than all the doctors in several years. The Romans didn't agree on the manner in which the bar should be: Cato wanted the board to be all bristling with points in order to tear the feet of the litigants, and Marcellus, to the contrary, that it be well protected against the sun's rays and time's injuries in order to invite everyone to come there and multiply the litigations.

The physicians heal and kill the sick here as everywhere in the world; when they approach a sick person, instead of diagnosing his illness they ask him what it is: there is no more certain medicine for a long and happy life than to send them away. A Latin poet, speaking about a young

Roman who went to sleep in good health, said that he died suddenly during the night because he had seen a physician in his dream. What I find unjust is that the doctor who kills and the one who heals are paid equally, and that there is no judge to punish an ignorant physician.

The most adroit exercise is that of certain thieves, called here *filoux;* their trade is more subtle than that of Geber; if he showed how to change lead into gold, they make gold out of nothing. They steal with such skill that, if it wasn't shameful to allow oneself to be robbed, it would be a pleasure to be by people so subtle and so crafty. Hercules would never have known who had taken his oxen if Cacus had been one of the *filoux* of Paris. To tell you the truth, whoever goes about by night is in danger of finding himself naked like our first parents, and whoever sleeps during the day often belies Aristotle, who says that there is no void in nature; for those who are not sufficiently wary find nothing, neither in their strongboxes nor in their houses. These thieves are always punished by the judges, but that is when they are trapped and don't exercise their craft skillfully.

The animals here are gentler than anywhere else in the world; one doesn't see snakes, nor almost any sort of poisonous creature. What is astonishing is to see that the horses, the most high-spirited of animals, here lose their boldness and become gentler than the asses of Arcady. The French do whatever they want to them; they come close to making them kneel down, like the Turks make the camels of their caravans do. They beat them, they castrate them, and, when they no longer know how to torment them, they reduce them to the ugly shape of a monkey by cutting off their tails and ears. From this comes the proverb that "Paris is the paradise of women, the purgatory of men, and the hell of horses."

As for piety, I have never seen a people more devout, priests more discreet, a clergy more disciplined, and the religious giving better example. The people frequent the churches with piety; the merchants go to ask God that their businesses prosper. Only the nobles and the great lords go there to divert themselves, to chat, and to woo, and sometimes one sees men enter with their boots on, without remembering the respect that the Mohammedans have who, before entering their mosques, leave their shoes at the door.

Although they live a long time here, nevertheless one almost never sees old people; the men have neither beards nor their own hair, and they cover with much care the defects of the years with the hair of others, giving them a perpetual youthfulness. Since the wig has been adopted, the heads of the dead and those of women are expensive, it being the vogue that the tombs and the women furnish the most beautiful ornament for the heads of men.

Everyone dresses with much neatness. Ribbons, mirrors, and lace are three items without which the French cannot live. Gold and silver have become so common, as I have already noted, that they shine on the clothes of all sorts of persons, and the excessive luxury has confused servant with master, and the scum of the people with those of the highest class. Everyone wears a sword, making them all soldiers, and Paris resembles the Utopia of Thomas More, where people could not be told apart.

This is the land of pleasure: the lovers hardly ever sigh, no one is tormented by jealousy, the French soldiers go to their deaths as an amusement, and afflicted people do not appear in public. Musicians are so numerous that from the grandest lady down to the meanest servant, and from the noblest cavalier to the lowest lackey, everyone sacrifices to Orpheus, that is to say that everyone sings, and more so in the public squares and gardens than in private houses. The French scoff at the philosopher [Aristotle] who remarks in his *Politics* that the poets have never made Jupiter sing, as if song were not worthy of a god.

Since everything is expensive in Paris, the dead themselves pay a tax for obtaining a place of burial; thus a man at the point of death is less troubled about dying than about paying the physician who is killing him and the priest who inters him.

The men of letters are here as numerous as the ignorant are in Constantinople. There are several academies where these honorable people go to discourse; the two most famous are that of the French language [Académie Française] and that of the Sciences [Académie des Sciences]. The last is composed of several philosophers more enlightened than the ancients, who discover new mysteries of nature every day; the other is a company of sublime spirits who teach the beauties of the language to the French and who have made the nation the most eloquent in the universe. The university is also a renowned academy where the youth are trained in the principles of the natural order, and the Sorbonne is a famous seminary where theology gives instruction in speaking about the mysteries of religion; from there emerge the leading men of Europe in science and virtue.

I have heard it said that the alchemists are here in as great a number as the cooks, but they only draw useless knowledge from their art. Five to six thousand of them can be counted, who will be rather wretched for receiving from their labors and their diligence only some smoke, the usual recompense that is given to its adherents by an art rich in hope, liberal in promises, and ingenious in pain and fatigue, whose beginning is lying; its middle, labor; and its end, asking for alms.

The booksellers and the printers hold first place among the mechanical arts; there is no city in the world where more new books are seen and where the difficulty of getting something printed is greater. Several people write on noble and interesting subjects, but they are almost all poor. Moral philosophy is mainly to the taste of the French; they write about it with much refinement. They translate and print also several books in Greek, Latin, Italian, and Spanish, a certain sign of the poverty of the authors, of the wealth of the booksellers, and of the great fruit produced by the application of men of letters. The booksellers enrich themselves without understanding the books that they sell, and it is of them that Quevedo says "that they are tormented in the next world for the works of others."

One finds in Paris everything that one can ask for, one finds it immediately, and the world provides no invention for tasting all the pleasures of life that are practiced here. The Peripatetics and the Stoics never labored so much to reform manners as do the cooks to satisfy the belly. There are always new sauces and unknown stews, and the French, tired of feeding on the usual meats, have found the means of softening the stripped bones of animals and of turning them into delicious food. One lives here at a high price; the bread is good, it is white, well made, and a single loaf is sometimes so big that it suffices to satisfy an entire family for several days, thus leading a wag to say that if that way of making large loaves of bread had been practiced in Judaea at the time of the Messiah, the five thousand Jews who were satisfied would have been more astonished by the oven than by the miracle.[2]

Nevertheless, although one may be in a city of such abundance, he who has nothing has nothing, that is to say that water and fire are forbidden to those who have no money,

[2] The Miracle of the Loaves and Fishes, recounted in all four Gospels.

as they were to criminals in Roman times. I don't think there is in the world a hell more terrible than to be poor in Paris, and to see oneself continually in the midst of all the pleasures without being able to taste any of them. Amongst this great abundance, one finds a great number of miserable souls who ask for alms in a manner as if they were singing; one sees them frozen with cold in winter, and in springtime they offer flowers in order to arouse compassion.

They believe here neither in sorcery nor in magicians, and rarely in people being possessed. Adultery passes for a gallantry, even in the minds of husbands, who tranquilly see their wives carrying on affairs, and they are right. It is a great folly of our jealous Italian men to plant honor in so fragile a place.

They sell all sorts of things, except the art of keeping a secret: the French say that that is the profession of a confessor, and that for them they only keep quiet about indifferent matters that are not confided to them, and which they feel no longing to talk about.

Civility is more studied in France than in the realm of China. It is practiced with much gracefulness among persons of quality; the bourgeois mix affectation into it and the lower classes perform it boorishly. Each makes of it an art after his fashion. One finds masters who demonstrate the ceremonies, and some days past I met a rather shapely woman in the street who offered to sell me some compliments, and to give them to me at a cheap price. This woman goes into homes, displays her merchandise, and earns enough to live on.

They love strangers; they come here from all corners of the world to see the king, who is a very well built and very accomplished prince. The French enjoy at the same time all the pleasures that can flatter the senses, except smell.

Since the king doesn't like scents, everyone makes it a necessity to hate them; the ladies pretend to faint at the sight of a flower. Thus the most fastidious persons refuse to indulge themselves in scents, which we Italians love so completely and which the Spanish and all the Asian nations esteem as so precious. In addition, being deprived of this pleasure, we are continually engulfed in the bad smells of the streets and in the stench of the sewers, which would be able to carry the ship of Ptolemy.[3]

There are several masters who teach foreign languages; Italian and Spanish are more in fashion than the others, and they have their votaries. The women in particular, curious to hear these two languages and to speak them, do not spare their pains, and they succeed. The histories of the times and the great events of the world are written here with great refinement. They also describe in the almanacs all the battles and captures of cities and all important actions that take place on sea and land, and they take care to embellish the description with several pleasing emblems and illustrations.

Every year they hold during Lent a famous fair, called the Foire Saint-Germain; it is in a large space all filled with shops, where a great number of merchants exhibit all the most beautiful and richest merchandise that is made in this great city. One also finds there all sorts of liqueurs, wines, and preserves, and all types of precious furniture are sold. The whole town goes there, but rather more for amusement than for shopping. The most artful lovers, the prettiest girls, and the most skillful thieves compose a continual crowd. There is no theft of a heart or theft of a purse that isn't performed there, and since the crowds are always

[3] The ship of Ptolemy IV (221–203 B.C.E.) built for display (420 feet long).

great and continuous, there occur some rather strange adventures of theft and gallantry. The purses have the same fate as the souls of Pythagoras, they pass from one to another by an invisible transmigration. The king used to come, but at present he comes no longer. The principal entertainment occurs at night, when an infinite number of lights, arranged in all the shops, renders the fair more brilliant and more magnificent, hides more easily the defects in women's faces, and lends to other pleasures a more agreeable and more delightful flavor.

The invention of illuminating Paris during the night by countless numbers of lights merits the coming of the most distant peoples to see what the Greeks and the Romans never thought of for the policing of their republics. The lights, enclosed in glass lanterns suspended in the air, and placed at equal distances, are in an admirable arrangement; they are all lit at the same time and burn throughout the night. This spectacle is so beautiful and so well arranged that Archimedes himself, if he were still alive, could not add to it anything more pleasing or more useful. These nocturnal fires provide an extreme benefit to all the people; they contribute to public safety, as do also several troops of men, some on foot and others on horseback, who go about all night long through the city in order to prevent murders, thefts, and killings, which used to be perpetrated with impunity under cover of darkness. This renders Paris (if you put aside the dreadful noise), the safest and the most delightful city in the universe.

I return to the famous garden of the Tuileries, whose beauty charms even the blind who go to walk there every day in summer. As it is fashioned for the pleasure of a great many people, all the efforts of art have been made to render it worthy of a great number of important persons who frequent it, of a great number of beautiful ladies who embellish it, and of an extreme quantity of honest people who are always strolling there. Entry is forbidden to servants and the rabble. It is very spacious, and almost capable of containing a large part of the people, if they came here at the same time. Situated on the bank of the Seine, the view of that river, of the hills, and of the neighboring countryside increases its beauty and its charms. The grand avenues, covered by a great number of trees, which produce only shadow, are suitable for people to promenade in, and when one is tired, one finds some seats in all the places for sitting down, along with theaters, labyrinths, and carpets of fresh grass on which to retire as in a pleasant wilderness. There one sees displayed in their costumes all that the town has to offer that is most handsome, and all that luxury can devise that is most delicate and most affecting. The ladies, with fashions always new, with their finery, their ribbons, their gems, and their pleasing ways of dressing, display, in their gold and silver fabrics, the continual applications of their magnificence. The men, for their part, as vain as the women, with their feathers and their light-colored wigs, go there to try to please and capture hearts; but often they themselves are snared, for Dianas are not lacking there who charm Endymions.

In this so very pleasant place, people banter, dally, talk about love, news, business, and war. They make decisions, criticize, dispute, deceive each other, and with that everyone has a good time. In the spring one sees several kinds of flowers, and the nightingales in summer seem to have chosen their residence there; with their resonant voice they sing of their loves and their plaints. One sees no sad face there, one is quiet, removed from the noise, one hears no mournful language; and I believe that it was in this charming garden that Armida was found disarming her Rinaldo and enchaining him.

This beautiful place is maintained at the king's expense, and no trouble is neglected to make it pleasant; the king has placed there a governor with many subordinate officers. The gates are always guarded. If there were a greater amount of water and some fine marble statues, the eyes would receive more pleasure and have nothing more to wish for.

I have never seen so many abbés, or those who more willingly wear the short habit, the small collar, and the light-colored wig. In truth, they are the ornament of Paris and the refuge of women in distress. Since they have refined minds, their conversation is more pleasant and more sought after; I have found among them persons who are the most obliging, the most civil, and the most discreet. It would be desirable that the large number of abbés be diminished, by striking from this honorable rank all those whose monasteries are in the concavity of the moon and in imaginary spaces.

Although the men are industrious and resourceful in their work, the women do not neglect to perform half of the labor; the most beautiful mind the shops in order to attract the buyers. As they are extremely well-dressed, with gracious voices and words, they never fail, as I said previously, to take all our money, even though we have no desire to make a purchase.

On the Pont-Neuf one finds a great number of people who pass out handbills: some replace teeth that have fallen out, others make glass eyes; some heal incurable diseases; this one claims to have discovered the hidden power of some medicinal plants or of some powdered stones to whiten and embellish the face; that one gives assurance that he makes old people young. You find those who remove wrinkles from the forehead and the eyes, who fabricate wooden legs to repair the injuries of bombs; in short, everyone has such a strong and continual attention to work that the Devil can only tempt people on holidays and Sundays.

Would you like to be a right-thinking man in Paris for only six months, and afterwards live as a criminal? Change neighborhood, and no one will know you. Would you like to live there all your life as an unknown? Go lodge in a house where there are eight or ten families: the one that will reside closest to you will be the last to know who you are. Have you an inclination to be all covered in gold today and tomorrow dressed in rough serge? No one will take notice, and you can walk through town dressed as a prince or a porter.

One Sunday I saw, in a single parish, sixty-five marriages performed. They say that there are here up to 4,000 oyster-sellers; that each day they eat 1,500 big oxen and more than 16,000 sheep, calves, or pigs, beyond a prodigious quantity of poultry and game. The people spend one million each year to amuse themselves at the opera and at the two theaters.

Fifty thousand houses have been counted, in each one of which the families are so numerous that they live from the garret to the cellar. They also count five hundred large streets, beyond an infinite number of small ones, ten public squares, several markets, seventeen city gates, nine bridges with as many faubourgs, and more than thirty hospitals. One sees a great number of churches, colleges, several beautiful public or private libraries, and a quantity of rich and singular collections, adorned with medals, paintings, and full of the finest rarities of Europe.

It is not the custom here to lend anything, and sometimes it is a sort of insult to offer money and borrow some;

one never offers lodgings in one's house to strangers, nor even to one's friends.

There is in each neighborhood a sort of judge, named a commissioner, who decides certain small disputes right away and who prevents noise and quarrels.

Those who are not French cannot stand that the men comb themselves publicly in the streets, that the women always carry a small mirror in their hands, and that they go about masked all year long. The young people divert themselves at all the bodily exercises, and especially at tennis, in a closed and covered place. The old men pass the time at dice, cards, and the telling of news, and the ladies play more usually than the men; they also make many visits and are regulars at all the theatrical plays.

What one usually finds in Paris are: many words given, but not kept; thanks received, which they take pleasure to forget; some madmen in the streets, and some locked up; but what is rarely seen is modesty and wisdom. There are idle people, sober persons, and men who are aged. It is very rare to find the timid and the scrupulous; but what is never seen and what one would wish with more earnestness is repose, privacy, and a true friend.

Chocolate, tea, and coffee, moreover, are extremely *à la mode;* but coffee is preferred to the two others as a remedy that is said to be most excellent against sadness. Also, recently, a woman, learning that her husband had been killed in battle: "Ah! how miserable I am!" she said, "Quick, bring me some coffee!" And she was immediately consoled.

I didn't know these past days whether they still ate bread; he who went out to buy some came back saying that twisted bread [*le pain tortillé*], that I liked, was no longer *à la mode.* It is fashion that is the real demon that always torments this nation to the point that they no longer love women the way they used to and the most prodigal men would look upon the most tender attachment as a crime.

They have worn the neckties so short that one scarcely sees them, and at this moment they attach them to the collar, from whence they hang like sausages from Bologna. The French no longer carry swords but scimitars. The Bolognese dogs [a type of pug lap-dog] are presently considered ugly and insupportable, and only those with a wolf's muzzle and clipped ears are caressed, and the more deformed they are, the more they are honored with kisses and embraces.

The wigs also have their fashion; they used to make them *à la françoise,* and now they wear them *à l'espagnole.* The small watches have been in great demand, and they are ridiculous today, and the largest are the most fashionable. I have even heard it said that they no longer make compliments in letters, but that a new fashion has been introduced, which is to seal, no longer with a single seal, but with three, for fear of wounding good manners.

My dear friend, let us pray to God with all our hearts that He give to this brave nation the spirit of peace, and that the martial furor that always agitates it changes into a salutary fashion that brings back peace and tranquillity throughout Europe.

In Paris, 20 August 1692.

V
NIKOLAI MIKHAILOVICH KARAMZIN

LETTERS FROM PARIS[1]

1790

INTRODUCTION

Far more is known about Nikolai Mikhailovich Karamzin (1766–1826) than about any of the previous writers on Paris included in this anthology, for Karamzin was a literary

[1] Extracts from *Letters of a Russian Traveler, 1789-1790*, trans. and ed. Florence Jonas (New York: Columbia University Press, 1957), pp. 179-255. About half of Karamzin's letters on his travels through Europe first appeared in installments in the *Moskovskii zhurnal* in 1791 and 1792; the complete set was later published as *Pis'ma russkogo puteshestvennika* (Moscow, 1797–1801), 6 vols.; a recent Russian edition was edited by Iurii M. Lotman, N.A. Marchenko, and Boris A. Uspenskii (Leningrad, 1984). The first English translation was made by Andreas Andersen Feldborg from the German edition of 1801–03: *Travels from Moscow through Prussia, Germany, Switzerland, France and England* (London: Braddock, 1803), 3 vols. A selection of Parisian letters from the Jonas edition (1957) is presented here. The notes to the text are by Karamzin. Some minor grammatical and orthographical changes have been made silently.

giant, the founder of Russian prose style and the leader of the Sentimentalist movement in Russian literature.

Karamzin was born in 1766 in Mikhailovka, Simbirsk province, on the middle Volga, the son of a retired army captain. He started reading at an unusually early age, and later attended private boarding schools in Simbirsk and Moscow (1775–81). This was followed by service in a guards regiment in St. Petersburg (1782–83). During these years Karamzin was acquiring foreign languages, including French and German, and in 1783 his first literary work was published, a poor translation of a piece by the German writer Salomon Gessner. Karamzin was then only seventeen. In 1784, he befriended a nobleman, Ivan Petrovich Turgenev (no relation to the great writer) in Simbirsk, where Turgenev was visiting to found a Masonic lodge. This meeting was decisive in Karamzin's life, for Turgenev advised Karamzin to move to Moscow, which he did in 1785. There Turgenev introduced Karamzin to a literary circle, centered on a Masonic lodge, which was led by the enterprising publisher Nikolai I. Novikov, whose firms published, *inter alia,* Russian translations of Milton, Bunyan, Young, and other English and Continental writers. For Karamzin, these Moscow years were a time of literary and philosophical education, the editing of a children's magazine, the writing of original poetry and prose, and translating from English, French, and German (including the first Russian rendering of Shakespeare's *Julius Caesar).* In May 1789, four years after his move to Moscow, Karamzin set forth on his European tour, from which he returned (by ship from London) in November, 1790.

The details of Karamzin's career after his return to Russia need not concern us here, but some milestones should be mentioned. He founded and edited the journal

Moskovskii zhurnal, in which appeared, in the course of its brief life (1791–92), some of Karamzin's travel letters and other pieces in a new style of Russian prose that established the Sentimentalist (pre-Romantic) movement. During the 1790s he wrote some famous short-stories, including *Poor Liza* and *Natalia, the Boyar's Daughter;* the *Letters* appeared in book form between 1797 and 1801. In 1803, he turned away from belles-lettres to embrace historiography, and, at his own request, was named Imperial Historiographer by Czar Alexander I. The fruit of this appointment was his unfinished *History of the Russian State* (1818–29, 12 vols.), which brought the story of Russia down to the end of the sixteenth century. He was elected to the Russian Academy in 1818 and died in St. Petersburg in 1826.

Karamzin sojourned in Paris for three months, from March 27 to late June 1790, a stage in a European grand tour that took him from Russia through northern Poland, Germany, Switzerland, France, and England in 1789–90 (he was then in his early twenties). His tour should be viewed in the context of Russian cultural history, for it was only during the eighteenth century and after, as a consequence of the reign of Peter the Great (r. 1682–1725), that Russians looked westward, to European, and especially French, culture as a model and that Russian citizens ventured forth from the motherland to visit the countries and capitals of the West.

Karamzin, by now fluent in French, arrived in the French capital during the first year of the Revolution (the Bastille had been stormed on July 14, 1789), and he has fascinating things to report about those times. He strolls down the Rue Saint-Honoré with an abbé who points out to him the large empty mansions deserted by *émigrés,* their brilliant salon life now extinguished; he observes Louis XVI and Marie-Antoinette in the Sainte-Chapelle and the dauphin in the Tuileries Garden; and he sits in the National Assembly and listens to Mirabeau arguing against a proposal by the French clergy. But these and other glimpses of the gigantic historical event that was unfolding around him are secondary to Karamzin's fascination with the city, the French people, and, especially, their musical and spoken theater.

Karamzin's letters are in fact diary entries, not actual letters written and dispatched to real individuals, and they introduce us to yet another genre of urban descriptive writing. Parisian diaries are preserved from 1400 on, and the earliest were kept by residents, not visitors. Of such diaries, the best known is the so-called *Journal d'un bourgeois de Paris,* written by an anonymous cleric during the years 1405-49. The author's purpose was to chronicle the very difficult political and daily conditions of those years, which coincided with civil war and English occupation. City description was certainly not a conscious aim of this writer, but some of his entries vividly portray civic events like religious processions, royal entries, and the death and burial of King Charles VI. Like all diaries, the events are recorded in temporal sequence, which imparts an immediate, eye-witness quality; the diary simply ends in 1449, probably because the author died.

Karamzin's "letters," however, strike us as carefully crafted literary miniatures rather than as traditional diary entries. Still, their generally short lengths contrast with Marana's extended essay in the guise of a letter, and their dated headings create a sense of movement in time. As a result of the chronological sequence, Karamzin's Parisian letters are placed between two bookmarks, that of arrival and departure. He first glimpses Paris from afar and then enters the city in a mood of heightened expectation; several months later he leaves for England with regret, hoping to return some day. Again, temporal sequence leads him in his first letter to his hotel rooms, so that the great monuments — traditionally discussed at the beginning of Parisian descriptions (cf. Jean de Jandun, Guillebert de Mets, and the Venetian secretary) — are relegated to a letter dated two months later.

Additionally, the diary/letter form permits Karamzin to change subject and mood within and between letters, and to discuss matters in almost random order (reminiscent of Marana), a strategy justified by the changing circumstances of each day. Most of all, the diary/letter permits (almost demands) a first-person narrative, a quality that jumps off Karamzin's pages from his very first sentence ("As we drew near Paris, I kept asking if we should soon see it"). We have previously glimpsed such subjectivity in Marana, but in Karamzin it is far more prominent, as he reveals to us his emotions, enthusiasms, thoughts, and even a headache, all frequently accentuated by a very free use of exclamation marks. This degree of subjectivity goes well beyond Marana, and contrasts markedly with the earlier selections in this anthology, which rarely depart from a classic objectivity and impersonality of auctorial voice. (One exception is the Venetian secretary's mention of how he mistook the Pont Notre-Dame for an ordinary street.) We may recognize in Karamzin's first-person presence and emotionalism the spirit of early Romanticism, which is also conveyed by his rapturous sharing of excitement with his epistolary "friends" and traveling-companion Bekker — a symptom of the early Romantic cult of friendship.

Other stylistic features in the letters are the recording of conversations (set in quotation marks), which imparts immediacy and liveliness, and especially, pictorialism. The latter device is immediately displayed in the first two letters when the author is orienting himself in his new environment. His evocative word-painting of the shops and garden of the Palais-Royal and the view of the city from the Porte de Versailles introduce a literary resource that we have not encountered before and that, in fact, is rarely found in Parisian descriptions before him.

Karamzin's literary style and devices remind us of the techniques of the novelist, and in this regard his preface to the German and English editions of 1801-03 is revealing:

> Much in my Letters is unimportant; much is trivial. I grant it; but, if we can forgive Richardson and Fielding for telling us that Grandison took tea twice a day with his dear Miss Biron, and that Tom Jones slept exactly seven hours at this or that inn, why should a traveler, who writes to his friends, be harshly treated for introducing many circumstances of inferior consequence? Nor can the man wrapped in his surtout, and carrying the pilgrim's staff, be expected to write with the elegance of a courtier, or the accuracy of a professor.
>
> For the rest, I would advise him who seeks in Travels only geographical and statistical information, rather to read Busching's *Geography,* than these Letters.

Karamzin reveals that he has read Richardson's *Sir Charles Grandison* (1753) and Fielding's *Tom Jones* (1749), the former an epistolary novel, a popular form in the eighteenth century. (The *Geography* [*Erdbeschreibung*] by Anton Friedrich Busching [1724–93] went through many Russian editions.) And he virtually says that the incidental details found in his *Letters* follow these models. Some modern critics have sought links between the *Letters of a Russian*

Traveler and eighteenth-century travel literature, such as Charles Dupaty's *Lettres sur l'Italie en 1785* (1st ed. 1788), which is mentioned more than once by Karamzin (although not in the Parisian pages). Whatever his precise sources, it seems certain that Karamzin enriched urban description by adopting some of the techniques of the novelist and travel writer of his day.

Karamzin's letters offer a wealth of observations on the Parisian experience. Of particular interest is his immediate reaction to the urban density and activity, which he had not encountered to such a degree in his previous travels:

> This indescribable hubbub, this wondrous diversity of objects, this extraordinary multitude, this unusual vivacity, struck me with a kind of wonder. I felt as though I had fallen, like a tiny grain of sand, into a terrible abyss and was spinning around in a vortex.

Karamzin had experienced Russian and European cities before Paris, but the scale and activity of the French metropolis overwhelmed him — a premonition of the dizzying effect of later modern cities upon their denizens and visitors and the attendant perceived reduction of the individual to a grain of sand or an insect.

Notable are Karamzin's pages devoted to the performances he witnessed at the various Parisian theaters. His literary culture led him there every evening during his first month, but his report about how even the poor people went to the theater several times a week is testimony to the growth of leisure time in the eighteenth century for all social classes and the increase in venues for entertainment. (Paris in 1790 had five main theaters, including the opera, in contrast to three in Marana's time, a century previous; in addition, as Karamzin notes, there were in 1790 many small theaters, in the Palais-Royal and along the boulevards.)

The descriptions of performances at the Opéra, at the other theaters, and at the Concerts Spirituels make for lively reading and are of real value to theater, ballet, and music historians of this period. These pages move us off the streets and into the life within buildings, as do Karamzin's pages on coffeehouses, the National Assembly, and more.

At one point he asks: "Which would be the most interesting account of Paris?" He considers an enumeration of its monuments, its objects of splendor and taste, and then says:

> But I would give up ten such accounts, even the most detailed, for one brief study or gallery of sketches of the worthy people in Paris, who live, not in the huge palaces, but for the most part in garrets, in some crowded corner, in obscurity.

He then proceeds to relate how three *Luftmenschen* earn their subsistence, and we believe his sympathetic accounts, which anticipate the nineteenth-century interest in the proletariat and the underclass, as expressed in its literature, art, and politics. His sympathy for the lower classes, characteristic of Russian intellectuals of his and later times, is apparent throughout his letters, which frequently remark upon the ubiquitous contrast of Parisian splendor and squalor.

Paris in the first year of the Revolution: No better description has ever been written.

Nikolai Mikhailovich Karamzin

Bibliography

Karamzin's extensive writings are supplemented by a considerable body of scholarly and critical studies on him and his works. A basic bibliography and concise summary of his achievement are given in Neil Cornwell and Nicole Christian, eds., *Reference Guide to Russian Literature* (London and Chicago: Fitzroy Dearborn, 1998), pp. 417–18 (entry by Anthony Cross).

Letters from Paris

Paris, March 27, 1790

As we drew near Paris, I kept asking if we should soon see it. Finally, there unfolded a vast plain, and covering its expanse — Paris! Our eager eyes turned toward this huge mass of buildings, and our gaze was lost in its heavy shadows. My heart throbbed.

"There it is," I thought. "There is the city which for so many centuries has been the model for all Europe, the fount of taste and fashion; the city whose name is pronounced with reverence by the learned and unlearned, philosophers and fops, artists and fools, in Europe and Asia, in America and Africa, whose name became known to me almost together with my own; the city about which I have read so much in novels, have so often dreamed, so often thought! There it is! I see it and soon shall be in it!"

Oh my friends! This moment was one of the happiest moments of my journey! Never have I approached a city with such curiosity, such impatience!

Indicating Paris with his walking stick, our French traveling companion said, "Here, on the right, you see the Faubourg Montmartre and the Temple; straight ahead, Saint-Antoine; and on the left, beyond the Seine, the faubourgs Saint-Marcel, Saint-Michel, and Saint-Germain. This lofty Gothic tower is the ancient cathedral of Notre-Dame. This beautiful new church, whose architecture must surely amaze you, is the church of Sainte-Geneviève, the protectress of Paris. There in the distance, with glistening dome, rises l'Hôtel Royal des Invalides, one of the largest buildings in Paris, where the king and the nation take care of deserving and aged veterans."

Soon we entered the Faubourg Saint-Antoine, but what did we see? Narrow, filthy, muddy streets, miserable houses, and ragged people.

"Can this be Paris," I thought, "the city which from afar appeared so splendid?"

The scene changed completely, however, when we reached the banks of the Seine. Here, there appeared before us beautiful buildings, houses six stories high, rich shops. What throngs! What color, what noise! Carriage racing after carriage, continuous shouts of: "Gare! Gare!" and the people surging like the sea.

This indescribable hubbub, this wondrous diversity of objects, this extraordinary multitude, this unusual vivacity, struck me with a kind of wonder. I felt as though I had fallen, like a tiny grain of sand, into a terrible abyss and was spinning around in a vortex.

After crossing the Seine, we stopped on Rue Guénégaud at the Hôtel Britannique. There on the third floor we found two light, clean rooms, for which we pay two louis d'or a month. The proprietress showered us with politeness. She ran about, bustled, designated the place for our beds, trunks, and suitcases, and accompanied each word she said with "Aimables étrangers!" (Amiable strangers, esteemed strangers). Our traveling companion, the merchant, wished us every possible pleasure in Paris, and left.

Within half an hour we finished eating and making our toilet. We locked our rooms, went out into the street, and mingled with the crowds which, like the waves of the sea, carried us to the famous New Bridge (Pont-Neuf), on which stands a magnificent statue of Henry IV, most beloved of French kings. Was I able to walk past it? No! My feet just would not move; my eyes just stared at the image of the hero, and I could not turn away for several minutes.

Leaving Bekker at the statue of Henry, I went to M. Bréguet, who lives near the New Bridge on the Quai des Morfondus [Quai de l'Horloge]. His wife received me and, upon learning my name, immediately brought me a letter — a letter from my dear ones! Imagine your friend's joy! You are well and happy! All anxiety disappeared in a moment. I became happy as a careless youth — read the letter ten times — forgot Madame Bréguet, and did not say a word to her — my soul at this moment was filled only with thoughts of my distant friends.

"You seem overjoyed," said my hostess. "It is pleasing to see this."

At this I came to myself and began to apologize awkwardly. I wanted to talk with her about Geneva, her birthplace, but could not, and finally left. Bekker saw me running; he saw the letter in my hand; he saw my face and was happy, for he loves me. We embraced on the Pont-Neuf, beside the monument, and it seemed to me that bronze Henry, watching us, smiled. Pont-Neuf! I shall never forget you!

My heart was contented and happy. I walked with Bekker through the streets of the unfamiliar city, with no guide, no purpose, no aim — and everything that met our eyes interested and pleased us.

The sun set. Night fell and the lamps were lighted in the streets. We arrived at the Palais-Royal, a massive structure which belongs to the duc d'Orléans and is called the capitol of Paris.

Just picture a beautiful square palace; and beneath it arcades, where in countless shops glitter treasures from all the world, riches from India and America, emeralds and diamonds, silver and gold; everything that Nature and Art have produced; all possible adornments of royal splendor; every luxury designed for life's delight! And all this, to attract the eye, is most wonderfully displayed and illuminated by bright, dazzling lights, of many colors. Just picture multitudes of people thronging these galleries, walking to and fro for the sole purpose of looking at one another! Here you see, too, the finest coffeehouses in Paris, also crammed with people. Here they read newspapers and magazines aloud, they shout, argue, make speeches, and so on.

My head was swimming. We left the galleries, and sat down to rest in a chestnut-lined walk of the Jardin du Palais-Royal. Here silence and a half-light reigned. Although the arcades shed their light upon the green boughs, it was lost among the shadows. From another walk floated soft, sweet sounds of tender music. A slight breeze stirred the tiny leaves of the trees. "Nymphs of joy" approached us one after another, threw flowers at us, sighed, laughed, invited us into their grottoes with promises of untold delights, and vanished, like phantoms of a moonlit night.

To me this seemed a magic spell, like the island of Calypso or the palace of Armida. I sank into a pleasant reverie.

Paris, April 2, 1790

"I am in Paris!" This thought produces in my soul a kind of peculiar, agitated, inexplicable, delightful sensation. "I am in Paris!" I tell myself as I dash from street to street, from the Tuileries to the Champs-Élysées. Suddenly I stop, I regard everything with heightened curiosity — the houses, carriages, people. That which was known to me from descriptions I am now seeing with my own eyes. I am rejoiced and gladdened by the living picture of the greatest, most famous city in the world, wonderful, unique for the diversity of its scenes.

Five days have passed like five hours, amid the tumult and crowds, at the theater, and in the enchanting Palais-Royal. My soul is filled with lively impressions, but I cannot explain them even to myself, and I am in no condition to tell you anything coherent about Paris. Let my curiosity be satisfied, and then there will be time to consider, describe, praise, criticize. Now let me only note what seems to be Paris's primary trait — the remarkable swiftness of the people's movements, the astonishing rapidity of their speech and actions. Descartes' vortex theory could have been conceived only by a Frenchman, a Parisian. Here everyone is hurrying somewhere; seemingly they are all trying to outstrip each other; they hunt out and snatch at ideas. They guess at what you want, so as to be rid of you as quickly as possible. How different they are from the solemn Swiss, for example, who always walk with measured steps and listen with an attentiveness that makes a shy and reserved person blush. Even when you have ceased speaking, they continue to listen and to weigh your words. How deliberately, how cautiously they reply, fearful that they have not understood you! The Parisian, on the other hand, is always trying to anticipate your wish. Before you have finished a question, he has answered you, bowed, and taken his leave!

Paris, April 1790

At first sight, when you enter it through the Porte de Versailles, Paris appears to be a most magnificent city. Before you, enormous buildings with lofty spires and domes; on the right, the River Seine with picturesque little houses and gardens; on the left, beyond the extensive green plain, the Montmartre, with its countless windmills, which, with their vanes rotating, take on the appearance of a flock of some sort of feathered giants, ostriches, or Alpine eagles. The road is wide, level, and smooth as a table, and in the evening it is usually illuminated by lamps. The gatehouse is a small building whose architectural beauty captivated us.

You drive through a wide velvety meadow into the Champs-Élysées, called by this attractive name not without reason — a small wood, planted by the oreads themselves, with tiny flower patches throughout which are scattered rude buildings. In one of these you will find a coffee-house, in another a shop. Here, on Sundays, the people stroll, music resounds, and the gay shop-keepers' wives dance. The poor people, exhausted from their week's toil, rest on the fresh grass, drink wine, and sing *vaudevilles.* You have not the time to take in all the beauties of this small wood, of these sweet little groves, which seem to be scattered at random on both sides of the road. Your glance is carried forward to a large, octagonal square, where there rises a statue of Louis XV surrounded by a white marble balustrade. When you reach it, you see before you the shaded walks of the famous garden, the Tuileries, which adjoins the majestic palace. A beautiful sight! Entering the garden, you do not know what to admire first, the thickly wooded walks, the charming high terraces which extend on both sides for the full length of the garden, or the beautiful pools, vases, groups, and statues. The artist Le Nôtre, designer of this garden, which is certainly the most artistic in Europe, stamped each part of it with the mark of his intellect and taste. It is not the common folk who walk here, as they do in the Champs-Élysées, but the so-called "best people," cavaliers and ladies, dripping powder and paint.

You ascend to the vast terrace, and look about to the right and left. Everywhere you see enormous buildings, palaces, churches — the beautiful banks of the Seine, with its granite bridges over which thousands of people swarm and scores of coaches rumble. You view everything and ask: What is Paris? It is not enough to call it the first city in the world, capital of splendor and enchantment. Stop here, if you do not wish to change your opinion, for if you go farther you will see crowded streets, an outrageous confusion of wealth and poverty. Close by a glittering jewelry shop, a pile of rotten apples and herrings; everywhere filth and even blood streaming from the butchers' stalls. You must hold your nose and close your eyes. The picture of a splendid city grows dim in your thoughts, and it seems to you that the dirt and muck of all the cities in the world is flowing through the sewers of Paris. Take but one more step, and suddenly the fragrance of happy Arabia or, at least, Provence's flowering meadows, is wafted upon you, for you have come to one of the many shops where perfume and pomade are sold. In a word, every step means a new atmosphere, new objects of luxury or the most loathsome filth. Thus you must call Paris the most magnificent and most vile, the most fragrant[1] and most fetid city.

Because of the enormity of the houses, every street without exception is narrow and dark. The famous Saint-Honoré is the longest, noisiest, and dirtiest of all. Woe to the poor pedestrian, especially when it rains! Either he must walk through mud in the middle of the street,[2] or be drenched by

[1] Because nowhere are such perfumes sold as in Paris. — N.K.

[2] The roadway in Paris is made with a slope on both sides of the street. As a result there is always terrible mud in the middle. — N.K.

water pouring from the roofs. Here a carriage is a necessity,[3] at least for us foreigners. The French manage by some miracle to walk through the mud without getting muddy. They jump skillfully from stone to stone, and take shelter in the shops from the galloping carriages. The renowned Tournefort, who had traveled almost the entire world, was crushed to death by a fiacre on his return to Paris, because on his travels he had forgotten how to leap in the streets, like a chamois — an art required of the local inhabitants!

Follow any straight line in the city in whichever direction you wish, and you will always find yourself in a thick shady avenue called a "boulevard." There are three lanes, one for carriages and the other two for pedestrians. The boulevards run parallel and form a magic ring or frame around Paris.

Here the Parisians formerly gathered to play with bowls (*à la boule*) on the green grass, from which originated the name "boulevard." Originally, where the *allées* are now, there used to be only one rampart, which protected the capital of France from enemy raids. The trees were planted much later.

One section of these boulevards is called "the old," and the other "the new." On the former you see examples of taste, riches, and splendor, everything that has been devised by idleness to engage the interest of idleness. Here is the Comédie, there the Opéra; here glittering palaces, there

3 One must pay about four rubles a day for a decent hired carriage. It is possible also to ride in fiacres, that is, cabs, which stand at every crossroad. True, they are not very fine either outside or inside. The coachman, in a shabby waistcoat or threadbare coat, sits on the coachbox, continually pressing not horses, but the skeletons of horses, which alternate between pulling and standing still — they run a little, then stop. You can ride from one end of the city to the other in such an equipage for twenty-four sous. — N.K.

gardens of the Hesperides, which lack nothing but golden apples. Here coffee-houses hung with green garlands; there a bower adorned with flowers like a rustic temple of love. Here a long row of carriages, out of which peep youth and antiquity, beauty and ugliness, wisdom and stupidity, in the most living, characteristic forms. And finally, a detachment of the National Guard marches by. I have spent an entire day in this busy part of the boulevards.[4]

The so-called "new section" of the boulevards affords quite a different sight. There the trees are shadier, the *allées* prettier, the air fresher, but there are few people. You hear neither the rattle of carriages nor the stamp of horses, neither songs nor music. You see neither English nor French fops, neither powdered heads nor rouged faces. Here the good artisan, with his wife and daughter, seeks rest in the thick shade. Here his son strolls slowly with his young bride. Here are fields of corn, rustic toil, industrious peasants. In short, here everything is simple, quiet, and peaceful.

But now let us return to the bustle of the city. Charles V said, "Lutetia, non urbs, sed orbis" (Lutetia [that is, Paris] is not a city, but the whole world). What would he say now, when his Lutetia has grown twice as large and twice as populous as it was in his day! Picture to yourself twenty-five

[4] Among the most magnificent houses in this section, I noted that of the famous Beaumarchais. This man has known not only how to turn the heads of the Parisian public with a novel comedy, but also how to amass an astounding fortune; not only how to expose artistically the weaknesses of the human heart, but also how to exploit these weaknesses to fill his purse.

He is at one and the same time a witty writer and a subtle and worldly man, an astute courtier and calculating merchant. Beaumarchais now has every means to enjoy life. Curious people come to look at his house as a marvel of wealth and taste. One bas-relief above the gates is worth thirty or forty thousand livres. —N.K.

thousand houses, four or five stories high, filled with people from top to bottom! In spite of all the geographical almanacs, Paris has a greater population than Constantinople or London, containing, according to the latest calculation, 1,130,450 inhabitants, including 150,000 foreigners and 200,000 servants. Go from one end of the city to the other. Everywhere there are crowds of people on foot and in carriages; everywhere noise and hubbub, in large and small streets, and there are about a thousand streets in Paris! At ten, at eleven o'clock at night there is still life, movement, noise everywhere. At one and two o'clock many people are still about. At three and four you hear the occasional rattle of a carriage. Yet these two hours can be called the quietest of all. At five the workmen, Savoyards, and artisans begin to appear in the streets, and little by little the whole city comes alive again.

At this point, would you like to look at the most famous buildings in Paris with me? No. Let us leave this for another time. You are tired, and so am I. I must change the subject — or conclude....

Paris today is not what it was. An ominous cloud hangs over its domes and dulls the brilliance of this once magnificent city. The golden splendor which once reigned here — in its favorite capital — the golden splendor, having veiled its sorrowful face, has ascended to the heavens and concealed itself behind the clouds. Only a pale ray of its radiance remains which, like the setting sun, glimmers faintly on the horizon. The terrors of the Revolution have forced the wealthiest inhabitants to flee. The most distinguished of the nobility have gone away to foreign lands, and those who have remained here live for the most part within the intimate circle of their friends and relations.

"Here," said Abbé N__, as we walked through Rue Saint–Honoré, indicating with his walking stick the large mansions which now stand empty, "here, on Sundays at the home of the Marquise de D__ assembled the most fashionable ladies of Paris, distinguished people, celebrated wits (*beaux esprits*). Some played cards, while others discussed their philosophy of life, the tender sentiments, pleasures, beauty, and taste. Here, on Thursdays, at the home of the Comtesse d'A__, the most thoughtful political thinkers of both sexes assembled, compared Jean-Jacques with Mably, and drew up plans for the new Utopia. There, on Saturdays, at the home of the Baronne de F__, M__ read his commentaries on the book of Genesis and explained to interested ladies the nature of ancient chaos, which he presented in such terrifying light that the listeners swooned from fright. You have come to Paris too late. The happy days are gone. The pleasant suppers have ended. The best people (*la bonne compagnie*) have scattered to the ends of the earth. The Marquise de D__ has gone to London, the Comtesse d'A__ to Switzerland, and Baronne F__ to Rome to take the veil. Now an honest man does not know where to go, what to do, or how to spend the evenings." However, Abbé N__ (to whom I brought a letter from his brother the Comte de N__ in Geneva) admitted to me that the French had long since forgotten how to enjoy themselves in society as they had in the time of Louis XIV, for example, in the homes of the famous Marion Delorme, the Comte de la Suse, or Ninon de Lenclos, where Voltaire composed his first verses; where Voiture, Saint-Evremond, Sarasin, Gramont, Ménage, Pellisson and Hénault sparkled with wit, sprinkled Attic salt on every conversation, and were the arbiters of amusement and taste.

"John Law," continued the abbé, "John Law with his unfortunate bank scheme destroyed both the wealth and amiability of the Parisians, transforming our pleasure-loving marquises into traders and usurers. Where formerly all the subtleties of the intellect were displayed, where the French tongue was drained of all its wealth, all its nuances, in pleasant jests and witty sayings, they now discuss the value of bank notes, and houses where the best people once gathered have been transformed into bourses. Circumstances changed — John Law fled to Italy — but since then true French gaiety has rarely appeared in Parisian gatherings. Horrible games were introduced. Young ladies came together in the evenings for the sole purpose of impoverishing one another. They flung cards right and left, and forgot the art of the Graces, the art of pleasing. Then the parrots and economists became the fashion, *Intrigues Académiques,* Encyclopedists, and *calembours* [puns], bringing with them magnetism, chemistry and dramaturgy, metaphysics and politics. Young beauties became authors and found a way to put even their lovers to sleep. Finally we talked of plays, operas, and ballets in mathematical terms and explained the beauties of *La Nouvelle Héloïse* numerically. Everyone philosophized, became over solemn, over subtle, and introduced into the language strange, new expressions which even Racine and Boileau would not have been able nor have wished to understand — and I do not know to what we would finally have resorted from boredom if the thunder of the Revolution had not suddenly crashed over us."

With this the abbé and I parted.

Yesterday I saw the king and queen in the royal chapel. The king's countenance bespoke composure, gentleness, and kindness, and I am certain that his soul is free of any wicked intent. There are fortunate people in the world who, by nature, cannot help loving good and doing good. This sovereign is such a man! He may be ill-starred, he may perish in the tumultuous storm, but impartial history will list Louis XVI among the beneficent rulers, and the friend of mankind will shed a sincere tear in his memory.

Despite all the blows of fate, the queen is beautiful and stately. She is like a rose which, even when chill winds blow, still retains its freshness and beauty. Marie was born to be a queen. Her air, her glance, her smile — all denote an uncommon soul. Her heart must be suffering, but she knows how to hide her sorrow, and not a single cloud is to be seen in her bright eyes. Smiling like the Graces, she leafed through her prayer book, glanced first at the king, then at the princess, her daughter, and again turned to the book. Elizabeth, the king's sister, prayed with great fervor and devotion. She seemed to be weeping.

The church was so crowded that I would have fainted from the heat and closeness had it not been for a lady who, observing my pallor, offered me her smelling salts. Everyone watched the king and queen, especially the queen. Some sighed, and dried their eyes with their white handkerchiefs; others only looked on indifferently and mocked the poor monks who were singing the vespers. The king was wearing a purple caftan, while the queen, Elizabeth, and the princess wore black dresses with simple headdress.

I saw the dauphin in the Tuileries. The lovely, gentle Lamballe, to whom Florian dedicated his fables, was leading him by the hand. Sweet child! Angel of beauty and innocence! He was wearing a dark waistcoat with a blue ribbon across his shoulders. How he romped and played in the fresh air! People came running from all directions to look at him, their heads bared. They all joyfully surrounded the sweet boy, who caressed them with his glance and his smiles. The French still love the royal family!

Paris, April [1790]

On Thursday, Friday, and Saturday of Holy Week there used to be a famous promenade in the Bois de Boulogne. I say "used to be," because the one I saw today could hardly be compared with those of former times. In those days the wealthy and the dandies ordered new equipages for the occasion, and four or five thousand carriages, each one finer, more splendid, more fashionable than the others, appeared before the eyes of the spectators.

I walked there and saw about a thousand carriages, but not a single splendid one. This promenade reminded me of our May First in Moscow. There was a line of carriages from the Champs-Élysées to the Abbaye de Longchamp. The people stood two rows deep by the side of the road, shouting and jeering indecently at the promenaders. For example: "Look! There goes that fishwife with her neighbor, the shoemaker's wife!" "Well, if that isn't the longest red nose in all of Paris!" "See that young coquette of seventy. Who can keep from falling in love with her?" "Just look at that chevalier de Saint-Louis with the young wife and the horns!" "There is the philosopher who sells his wisdom for two sous!"

Young dandies pranced along on English horses, looked into each carriage and mocked the mob, "Allons, allons, mes amis de l'esprit, de l'esprit bon; c'est de la vraie gaieté Parisienne!" [Come on, come on, my spirited friends, of good spirit; this is the true Parisian gaiety!]

Others strolled about carrying wooden sabers, in place of walking sticks, "pour se confondre avec le peuple" [in order to mingle with the people].

It was the priestesses of Venus, however, who distinguished themselves above all. They rode in the very finest carriages.

One young actress had astonished her acquaintances by breaking off with a handsome young man, Count D__. When asked why she had done this, she replied, "Why are you so surprised? He is a monster, a tyrant. He would not even give me a new carriage for the promenade at the Bois de Boulogne. I was obliged to give the preference to an old marquis who pawned all his wife's jewels to buy me the most expensive carriage in Paris!"

Paris, April 29, 1790

I spent all of today sitting alone in my room, nursing a headache, but when it began to grow dark, I walked to the Pont-Neuf. Resting against the statue of Henry IV, I watched with great delight the shadows of night mingle with the dying light of day, the stars in the heavens and lamps in the streets begin to shine. Since I arrived in Paris, I have spent every evening, without exception, at the theater and that is why for nearly a month I have not seen the twilight. How fine it is in the spring, even in noisy, unattractive Paris!

I have gone to the theater every day for the entire month! And I have not yet had my fill of Thalia's laughter or Melpomene's tears! Each time I find new enjoyment. I myself am amazed; still, this is the truth.

It is also true that till now I lacked an adequate conception of the French theater. Now let me say that it has attained the greatest perfection possible and that here each part of the performance contributes to an harmonious whole which affects the spectator's heart in a most pleasing manner.

The five leading theaters in Paris are: the Opéra, the so-called "French Theater" (les Français), the Italian (les Italiens), the Theater of the Count of Provence (Théâtre de Monsieur), and Variétés. Performances are given every day, and every day (you may marvel at the French!) they are so crowded that by six o'clock you can scarcely find a place anywhere.

A person who has been in Paris, say the French, and has not seen the Opéra is like someone who has been in Rome and has not seen the Pope. Indeed, the Opéra is something extremely magnificent, mainly in its glittering decor and excellent ballet....

The [Opéra] orchestra, composed of the finest musicians of Paris, is a perfect match for the ballet and singers. In short, dear friends, here the Arts triumph in all their perfection. All this fills the spectator with a feeling which, without exaggeration, might be called rapture.

The expense of such a theater is, of course, very great. Even though one pays two to three rubles (in our money) for the boxes and parquet, even though these expensive places are always filled, the Opéra still costs the Court, according to Necker, about three or four millions a year....

[Karamzin attends the French Theater and sees the famous actor Jean Maudit de Larive in Voltaire's *Oedipe*.]

I saw him. What an awful crowd! Not only were the parquet, boxes, and parterre jammed, but even the orchestra was filled with spectators, to whom the musicians had yielded their places. At five o'clock, an impatient stamping and tapping began. At half-past five, the curtain rose and all became quiet. Oedipus does not appear in the first scene — silence reigned. But no sooner had Dimas said: "Oedipe en ces lieux va paraitre" [Oedipus is going to appear in this place], than thunderous applause broke out, which continued until the very moment when Larive appeared, in magnificent white Grecian robes, with blonde hair flowing over his shoulders. With a proud yet modest bow of the head, he expressed his gratitude to the spectators. The tumultuous acclaim continued through all five acts. Larive strained all his powers to be worthy of it and, as the French say, he surpassed himself in his art without sparing his poor lungs. I do not understand how he was able to hold out until the end of the tragedy. I do not understand how it was that the spectators did not grow weary from applauding. During the scene where Oedipus learns that he is the slayer of his father and the husband of his mother, learns this and curses fate in a terrifying way,[5] I became almost numb. No brush could portray the rage expressed on Larive's face at that moment: terror, anguish, despair, anger, bitterness, and everything, everything that I cannot express in words.

The audience sighed when, tormented and driven by the Furies, Larive rushed from the stage and bashed his head against the peristyle until all the columns shook. His groans were heard in the distance. The audience could not get enough of their Oedipus and, at the end of the play, they called poor Larive back to the stage. The actress Raucourt, who played the role of Jocasta, held him by the

[5] In the following lines:

Un Dieu plus fort que moi m'entraînait vers le crime;
Sous mes pas fugitifs il creusait un abîme;
Et j'étais, malgré moi, dans mon aveuglement,
D'un pouvoir inconnu l'esclave et l'instrument.
Voilà tous mes forfaits; je n'en connais point d'autres.
Impitoyables dieux, mes crimes sont les vôtres,
Et vous m'en punissez? Où suis je? Quelle nuit
Couvre d'un voile affreux la clarté qui nous luit?
Ces murs sont teints de sang; je vois les Euménides

arm. He could scarcely speak, and was on the point of collapsing when the curtain fell....

In addition to these five principal theaters there are a great many others in the Palais-Royal and on the boulevards, and each play has its particular audience. Not only the rich people, who live only for pleasure and amusement, but even the poorest artisans, Savoyards and peddlers consider it a necessity to go to the theater two or three times a week. They weep, laugh, applaud, whistle, and decide the fate of plays. Indeed, among them are the connoisseurs who take note of each, well-phrased thought of the author, each felicitous expression of the actor. "A force de forger on devient forgeron" [Practice makes perfect] — and often I am amazed at the unerring taste of the parterre, which is filled for the most part with people of low station. The Englishman triumphs in Parliament and the Exchange, the German in his study, the Frenchman in the theater.

Secouer leur flambeaux, vengeurs des parricides.
Le tonnerre en éclats semble fondre sur moi;
L'enfer s'ouvre.... [Voltaire, *Oedipe,* V. 4] — N.K.

[A god more powerful than I led me towards the crime;
Under my fleeting steps he hollowed out an abyss;
And I was, despite myself, in my blindness,
The slave and the instrument of an unknown power.
There you have all my horrible crimes; I do not know about any others.
Pitiless gods, my crimes are yours,
And you punish me for them? Where am I? What night
Covers with a frightful veil the brightness that illuminates us?
These walls are stained in blood; I see the Furies
Shaking their torches, avengers of parricides.
Bursts of thunder seem to engulf me;
Hell opens....]

The theaters in Paris are closed for only two weeks in the year, that is, during Easter. But how do the French manage to live even fourteen days without any public entertainment? During this period there is a Spiritual Concert (*Concert Spirituel*) every evening at the opera house, where the finest virtuosi display their art. I have spent some utterly delightful and, I may say, sweet hours there listening to Haydn's *Stabat Mater*, Jommelli's *Miserare*, and other works. Several times my breast was washed with warm tears — I did not wipe them away — I did not feel them. Heavenly music! While enjoying you, my spirit is lifted up, and I do not envy the angels. Who can prove to me that my soul, attuned to such holy, pure, ethereal joys, has not within it something divine, imperishable? Can these tender sounds, blowing like a zephyr on my heart, be the food of a crude, mortal being?

But nothing in this concert moved me so deeply as a beautiful duet by Lais and Rousseau. They sang — the orchestra was silent — the audience scarcely breathed — incomparable!

Paris, May [1790]

True, dear A. A., Paris is a unique city. Probably nowhere save here can one find so much material for philosophical contemplation. Where else are there so many objects of interest to one who values art, where else so many diversions and amusements? But where, too, are philosophy, and, most of all, the heart of man, exposed to so many perils? Here thousands of traps have been set for every weakness.... A tumultuous ocean, whose raging waves toss you from Charybdis to Scylla, from Scylla to Charybdis! The sirens are many, and their singing so sweet, so soporific. How easily one forgets oneself, one falls asleep! Waking, however, is almost always bitter, and the first object you see is your empty purse.

You must not think, though, that it is very expensive to live pleasantly in Paris. On the contrary, here a person can indulge all his tastes at small expense. I am speaking strictly of legitimate pleasures. If one would like to cultivate intimately singers and actresses, frequent gambling houses, and accept all invitations, then he needs the wealth of an Englishman. It is also expensive to live at home, that is, more expensive than in Moscow. But this is how you can pass the time very agreeably without spending much money: You can have a good room in the best hôtel.[6] In the morning you read various journals and newspapers, where you always find something entertaining, sad, or comical, while drinking coffee unlike any in either Germany or Switzerland. Then you call the barber, a chatterbox and liar who tells you a lot of amusing nonsense about Mirabeau and Maury, Bailly and Lafayette, smears your head with perfumes from Provence, and sprinkles you with a very fine white powder. After this you put on a simple, clean frock coat and wander about the city. You take in the Palais-Royal, Tuileries, and Champs-Élysées, where you visit some famous writer or artist, or a shop where they sell prints and pictures, or drop in at Didot's to admire elegant editions of the classics. For dinner you go to a restaurateur,[7] where for about five or six rubles, you are served well-prepared dishes and dessert.

[6] A hôtel is a lodging house where you have only a room and servant. Coffee and tea are brought from the nearest coffeehouse and dinner from an inn. — N.K.

[7] In Paris the proprietors of the best eating houses are called "restaurateurs." They give you a list of all the dishes with their prices. After making your selection, you eat at a small, private table. — N.K.

You consult your watch and arrange your time until six, so that, having viewed some church, adorned with monuments, or a picture gallery, library, or cabinet of rare objects, you may arrive at the Opéra, a comedy, or a tragedy, with the first stroke of the bow. Here you are captivated by the music and dancing. You laugh, you cry and, after the performance, weary but feeling pleasant and contented, you refresh yourself in the Palais-Royal, in the Café de Valois, or Café du Caveau, with a cup of *bavaroise.*[8]

You gaze at the magnificently illumined shops, arcades, and garden walks. Now and then you eavesdrop on some profound dabblers in politics. Finally you return to your quiet room, collect your thoughts, write a few lines in your diary, fling yourself on a soft bed and, with pleasant thoughts of the future, sink into a deep sleep (as both our day and life usually end).

Thus I spend the time, and I am contented.

Let me say a few words about the most important buildings of Paris. The Louvre at first was nothing but a dreadful fortress where the descendants of Clovis lived, and where rebels, disobedient barons who often rose up against their kings, were imprisoned. Francis I, who passionately loved to wage war, captivate fair ladies, and build magnificent castles, had the Gothic towers torn down, and erected in their place a huge palace, decorated by the best artists of his time. It was not inhabited until the time of Charles IX.

When Louis XIV ascended the throne, the Arts and Sciences ascended with him and, at a nod from the king, the Louvre was crowned with its magnificent colonnade, the

[8] An aromatic syrup with tea. — N.K.

finest creation of French architecture. But, what is even more surprising, it was built, not by a famous architect, but by Dr. Perrault, whom the derisive Boileau defamed and scolded in his satires. One cannot view without a kind of awe the peristyles, porticoes, pediments, pilasters, and columns. The roof is a terrace with a beautiful balustrade.

Each time that I stop opposite the main gates, I look and think, "How many millennia have flashed by the globe into eternity from the first interlaced boughs, which sheltered the son of uncivilized Adam from foul weather, down to the gigantic colonnades of the Louvre, marvel of vastness and taste! How small is man and yet how great his mind! How slow the achievements of man's mind, yet how varied and infinite!

Louis XIV lived in the Louvre a long time. Later he gave preference to Versailles, and Apollo and the Muses replaced the great monarch. Here are the academies.[9] Here, too, lived noted scholars, authors, and poets, worthy of the king's consideration. In yielding his dwelling place to Genius, Louis exalted both Genius and himself.

Speaking of the Louvre, one cannot forget the snow obelisk which the poor fashioned in the severe winter of 1788 [1784?] opposite the king's window, as a mark of their gratitude to him for having brought them firewood. All the poets of Paris wrote inscriptions for this unusual monument, the best of which was:

> Louis, the destitute whom your goodness protects
> Can only erect to you a monument of snow.
> But it pleases your generous heart more
> Than marble paid for with the bread of the unfortunate.

[9] There, in the hall of the Academy of Art, I saw four famous paintings by Le Brun representing the battles of Alexander the Great [now in the Louvre]. — N.K.

To memorialize this touching occurrence, a certain rich M. Joubot erected a marble obelisk before his house, near the Tuileries, on which are found all the inscriptions of the snow monument. I went to M. Joubot's to read them and, imagining how the French now treat their king, I could not help thinking, "Here is a monument of gratitude which demonstrates the ingratitude of the French!"

The name of the Tuileries comes from *tuile,* meaning the tile which used to be made here. The palace of the Tuileries, built by Catherine de Médicis, consists of five pavilions and four *corps de logis.* It is ornamented with marble colonnades, *frontons,* statues and, finally, an image of the radiant sun, emblem of Louis XIV.

The appearance of the building is not majestic, but it is pleasing. The situation is very fine — on one side, the River Seine and, in front of the main façade, the Tuileries Garden with its high terraces, flowers, pools, statues, and (best of all) its ancient, dense *allées* through which is visible, at a distance, on a vast square [Place Louis XV, later Place de la Concorde], a statue of Louis XV.

Although the Tuileries is at present occupied by the royal family, I saw its interior. On Whitsunday [May 23] the king and his retinue went to church. Behind them walked the queen and her ladies. The courtiers wore knights' mantles, the ladies rich robes. As soon as the king had passed, the curious onlookers ran into the inner chambers — I behind them — from hall to hall, and even to the sleeping quarters.

"Where are you going, gentlemen? What do you wish?" inquired the king's lackeys.

"To look about," replied my companions, as they continued on.

The rooms are decorated with Gobelin tapestries, paintings, Gothic statues, bronze fireplaces. However, my attention was taken up not only with things, but also with people — the ministers and ex-ministers, the royal servants who, on seeing the boisterous behavior of the slovenly young people, shouting and running about, only shrugged their shoulders. I myself felt sad as I walked behind them. "Was this once the brilliant French court?"

Seeing two people whispering, I imagined that they must be discussing the unhappy state of France and the dreadful disaster that probably awaits it!

The Tuileries is joined to the Louvre by a gallery which, for length and magnitude, has no equal in the world. Here it is intended to establish a royal museum or collection of paintings, statues, and antiquities now scattered in various places.

The Luxembourg belongs at present to the count of Provence [later Louis XVIII]. It is a majestic palace which was built by Marie de Médicis, wife of a great king, mother of a weak one, a woman ambitious of power but born without any talent for ruling. Long the Xanthippe of Henry IV, she succeeded him on the throne but to waste the fruits of Sully's economy, introduce civil war into France, and elevate Richelieu, only to become the victim of his ingratitude. After showering millions on her undeserving favorites, she died in exile, in poverty, with scarcely a piece of bread with which to satisfy her hunger or rags to cover her nakedness.

The ways of fate are sometimes horrible. With such thoughts I contemplated the beautiful architecture of this palace, its terraces and pavilions. For a few coins I was shown its interior. The rooms scarcely deserve notice, but here is the celebrated Rubens gallery, where this Raphael of the Netherlands poured out all the vigor of his art and his genius. It contains twenty-five large paintings of Henry IV and Queen Marie with numerous allegorical figures.

The Luxembourg Gardens were once the favorite promenade of the French writers. In its dense, dark *allées* they deliberated the meaning of their works. Here Mably often walked with Condillac. Hither, too, sorrowful Rousseau sometimes came to pour out his heart. Here the youthful Voltaire often sought harmonic rhythms for his keen thoughts and ideas and the gloomy Crébillon pictured to himself the wicked Atreus. Today the gardens are no longer what they were. Many avenues of trees have disappeared, have been cut down, or have withered. Nevertheless I often rest beneath the remaining trees, walk about alone or, sitting on the grass, read a book. Luxembourg is not far from the Rue Guénégaud, where I live....

The Palais-Royal is called the heart, soul, brain, essence of Paris. It was built by Richelieu who later presented it to Louis XIII, after inscribing on the gates: "Palais-Cardinal." This inscription displeased many people. Some called it arrogant, others senseless, pointing out that it is impossible to say "Palais-Cardinal" in French. There were some who supported Richelieu. They wrote and carried on public discussions, and Balzac, a celebrated connoisseur of the French language (of that period), of course, played a considerable role in this important debate, all of which proves that the intellects of Paris have long engaged in blowing bubbles! [The Queen-Mother Anne of Austria] ended this dispute by ordering "Cardinal" to be effaced and replaced by "Royal." Louis XIV was brought up in the Palais-Royal, and afterward presented it to the duc d'Orléans.

I shall not describe the exterior of this square palace, which is undoubtedly the largest building in Paris and which combines all the architectural orders. I shall speak only of its distinguishing features.

The family of the duc d'Orléans occupies only a very small part of the first floor. All the rest is given over to the enjoyment of the public and profit of the owner. Here are the playhouses, clubs, concert halls, stores, coffeehouses, taverns, and shops. Here rich foreigners engage rooms; here brilliant nymphs of the first class reside; here the lowliest also nestle. Everything that can be found in Paris (and what cannot be found in Paris?) is in the Palais-Royal. Do you need a fashionable frock coat? Come here, and you will find it. Do you wish your rooms magnificently decorated in a few minutes? Come here, and it will be done. Would you like paintings or prints by the finest masters, in frames? Come here, and choose. All kinds of precious things, silver, gold, are to be found here for silver and gold. Say the word and suddenly you will find in your study a choice library in all languages, in beautiful bookcases. In short, should an American savage come to the Palais-Royal, in half an hour he would be most beautifully attired and would have a richly furnished house, a carriage, many servants, twenty courses on the table and, if he wished, a blooming Laïs who each moment would die for love of him. Here are assembled all the remedies for boredom and all the sweet banes for spiritual and physical health, every method of swindling those with money and tormenting those without it, all means of enjoying and killing time. One could spend his entire life, even the longest, in the Palais-Royal and, as in an enchanting dream, dying, say: "I have seen and known all!"

Paris, May [1790]

Suleiman Aga, the Turkish Ambassador to the court of Louis XIV, first introduced coffee into France in the year of 1669. A certain Armenian named Pascal conceived the idea of opening a coffeehouse. The novelty gained favor, and Pascal accumulated a fair amount of money. After his death, the fashion of coffee drinking began to pass. Finally Pascal's heirs no longer had any customers. Some years later a Sicilian named Procope opened a new coffeehouse near the Théâtre Français, decorated it tastefully, and found a way of attracting the best people of Paris, especially writers. Fontenelle, Jean-Baptiste Rousseau, Saurin, Crébillon, Piron, and Voltaire gathered here, read prose and poetry to each other, argued, displayed their wit, and discussed the news of the day. Out of boredom, the Parisians went there to listen to them. This coffeehouse still bears Procope's name, but it has lost its former renown.

Could there be a happier thought than this one? You grow tired from wandering about the streets and want to rest. You enter a nice clean hall where, for a few kopecks, you can refresh yourself with lemonade or ices, read the newspapers, hear tales and discussions. You yourself talk and even declaim with no fear of annoying the proprietor. In the fall and winter, people who are not rich find here a pleasant refuge from the cold. There is a fireplace with a bright fire, before which they can sit as at home, paying nothing, and in addition enjoy the pleasure of society. Vive Pascal! Vive Procope! Vive Suleiman Aga!

Now there are more than six hundred coffeehouses in Paris (each with its own coryphaeus, wits, and windbags) but only about ten are considered famous. Of these, five or six are in the Palais-Royal, among them the cafés de Foi, du Caveau, de Valois, de Chartres. The first is beautifully furnished, while the second is adorned with marble busts of composers whose operas have captivated Parisian audiences — Gluck, Sacchini, Piccini, Grétry, and

Philidor. Here, too, is a marble plaque with the following gold inscription: "Two subscriptions were opened on this table: the first on July 18 to repeat the experiment of Annonay; the second on August 29, 1783 to render homage by means of a medal to the discovery of MM. de Montgolfier." On the wall hangs a medallion bearing a portrait of the two brothers Montgolfier.

Jean-Jacques Rousseau brought fame to one coffeehouse, le Café de la Régence, by playing chess there every day. Such crowds came to see this great writer that the *lieutenant de police* had to post a guard at the doors. Even today the ardent Jean-Jacquists still gather there to drink coffee in honor of Rousseau's memory. The chair on which he used to sit is kept as a curiosity. I have been told that one of the philosopher's admirers offered five hundred livres for it, but the proprietor would not sell it.

MEDLEY

I wanted to see how the people of Paris amuse themselves, so today I went to the *guinguettes.* This is the name given country inns where the common people gather on Sunday to eat for ten sous and drink very cheap wine. You cannot imagine how noisy and motley the scene was! The enormous rooms were crowded with men and women, shouting, dancing, and singing. I saw two sixty-year-old men solemnly dance the minuet with two old women. The young people applauded and shouted, "Bravo!" Some were staggering from the heady effects of the wine, but they, too, tried to dance, and almost fell down. They grabbed the wrong partners but, instead of apologizing, only muttered, "Diable! Peste!"

"C'est l'empire de la gross[e] gaieté." And so it is not only the Russian populace who worship Bacchus! The difference is that a drunken Frenchman makes a lot of noise, but does not fight.

At the doors of every *guinguette* stand flower girls, who seize you by the hand and say, "Kind sir, excellent sir! Let me give you this bouquet of roses." You must accept the gift without hesitation, show your gratitude with six kopecks and add a polite word. For the Parisian flower girls are of the same stamp as the [fishwives], and woe to those who do not please them — they would as soon cover you with mud. But if you keep the bouquet in your hand, they will not offer you others. Once on the Pont-Royal, two flower girls stopped the Baron and myself and demanded — a kiss! We laughed and tried to pass by, but the cruel Bacchantes kissed us vigorously on the cheek, roared with laughter, and shouted after us, "One more kiss! One more kiss!"

While walking along the Rue Dauphine, I noticed two Chinese pavilions on the river, which I recognized to be public baths. I went down, paid twenty-four sous, and bathed with cold water in a splendid little cabinet. The cleanliness was surprising. A special pipe conveys water from the river into each cabinet. People can also learn to swim here for thirty sous a lesson. Three men were swimming remarkably well while I was there.

There are also warm baths in Paris, where doctors often send their patients. The finest and most expensive are the Russian Baths, "Bains Russes, de vapeur ou de fumigations, simples et composés." For two rubles you are washed, rubbed dry with a sponge, and perfumed, just as in our Georgian baths.

I paid a visit to the Hôtel-Dieu, the main hospital in Paris, where patients of all faiths and nationalities are accepted, whatever their disease. At times there are as many as five thousand patients, under the care of eight doctors and one hundred assistants. One hundred and thirty nuns of the Augustinian order serve the unfortunates and see that cleanliness is observed. Twenty-four priests are on hand continually to administer Extreme Unction and pray for the dead. I saw so much in two wards that I could go no farther. I became ill. The groans of the sick rang in my ears until evening.

In spite of the good care, two hundred and fifty out of a thousand die. How can they set up such hospitals in the middle of the city? How can they drink water from the Seine, polluted as it is with all the filth from the Hôtel-Dieu? Horrible thought! Fortunate is he who leaves Paris healthy! I shall hurry to the theater to treat my melancholy and the beginning of a fever.

The Royal Library here is the finest in the world — at least, so the librarian told me. It consists of six tremendous halls crammed with books. Works by mystics occupy a space two hundred feet long and twenty feet high, scholastics one hundred and fifty feet, jurisprudents forty sagenes,[10] historians eighty sagenes. The volumes of poetry number forty thousand; the romances six thousand; books of travel seven thousand. In all, the library contains more than two hundred thousand volumes and sixty thousand manuscripts. The system here is remarkable. You ask for a book, and within a few minutes it is in your hands. Since I am Russian, I was shown a Slavonic Bible and our empress's *Nakaz.*[11]

[10] A Russian measure; one sagene equals seven English feet.
[11] *Instructions,* Catherine the Great's radical reformist tract of 1766.

Charles V inherited twenty books from King John. Being fond of reading, he increased the number to nine hundred and founded this library. In a cabinet of ancient and modern coins, I studied with great curiosity the shields of the two most illustrious generals of antiquity — Hannibal and Scipio Africanus.[12] What pleasant recollections we owe to history! I was eight or nine years old when I first read about the Roman and, imagining myself a little Scipio, I held my head high. Since that time I have loved him as my hero. I despised Hannibal during the happy days of his fame, but on that decisive day, before the walls of Carthage, my heart almost wished him the victory. When all the laurels on his head had faded and died, when he wandered from land to land seeking shelter from the vengeful Romans, I became a tender friend of the great, though unfortunate, Hannibal and an enemy of the cruel Republicans.

They still preserve in the library two arrows of the American savages, tainted with a poison so potent that, if you should penetrate with them the blood of any living thing, it will stiffen and die within a few minutes.

In a hall on the ground floor stand two globes of such extraordinary size that the upper parts of them pass through the ceiling into the second story. They were made by the monk Coronelli.

The library's collection of engravings is also worthy of note.

There are many other public and private libraries in Paris, which are open to the public on specified days. Here you may read or copy whatever you wish. Nowhere in the world is there a second Paris for the learned or the inquisitive. Everything is at hand — only to be used!

[12] This is indicated by the inscription. — N.K.

The Royal Observatory, constructed without wood or iron, is in the form of a large rectangle with each façade facing one of the principal points of the compass. The meridian, which crosses France from north to south, from Collioure to Dunkerque, passes through a large hall on the ground floor. One room, called "La Salle des Secrets," presents a curious phenomenon. If you press your lips against a pillar and whisper a few words, they can be heard by a person standing at a distance near an opposite pillar, but a person who stands between you hears nothing. The monk Kircher wrote an explanation of this strange phenomenon.

Beneath the Observatory is a labyrinth which is used for various meteorological experiments. No one is permitted to visit it without a guide and torches. Three hundred and sixty steps lead you into this abyss. The darkness is frightening. The thick, damp atmosphere almost stops your breathing. I was told that two monks dropped behind while going down with some others who wanted to see it. They tried to catch up, but their torch went out. They searched in vain for a way out of the dark passageways. Eight days later they were found in the labyrinth, dead.

Paris, May [1790]

I am now wondering: Which would be the most interesting account of Paris? An enumeration of its monuments (scattered, as it were, throughout the streets), of various kinds of curiosities and objects of splendor and taste, undoubtedly has its merit. But I would give up ten such accounts, even the most detailed, for one brief study or gallery of sketches of the worthy people in Paris, who live, not in the huge palaces, but for the most part in garrets, in some crowded corner, in obscurity.

This is a vast field in which to collect a thousand interesting anecdotes! Here poverty, the lack of means of subsistence, drives people to amazing cunning, exhausts both reason and imagination! Here many people who have not a kopeck of certain income appear every day on the boulevards, in the Palais-Royal, even at the theater, in black caftans, their hair dressed and powdered, carrying a large purse and a long sword. Yet they live, they enjoy themselves and, judging from their outward appearance, are as carefree as the birds of heaven. And the means of living? They are diverse, without number, and known nowhere except in Paris.

For instance, there is a fairly well-dressed man, rather pleasing in appearance, who sits every day in Café de Chartres over his *bavaroise.* He talks continuously, jokes, tells amusing anecdotes, and do you know how he lives? By selling the placards or printed notices that are posted on the walls here. At night, after the city has settled down and the people have gone home, he walks from street to street, gathering his fodder. He strips the walls of the printed sheets and takes them to the pastry cooks who need the paper. For this he receives a few kopecks, a livre or two, or even a whole *écu.* Then he returns to his straw mattress in some *grenier* and falls asleep more peacefully than many a Croesus.

Another man who likewise is seen every day in the Tuileries and the Palais-Royal and who, by his dress, might be taken for a clerk, is a farmer-general. But I ask you to guess what kind? He farms — all the pins lost by the ladies in the Italian Theater. Just as the curtain is lowered and all the spectators are leaving the hall, he appears in the theater and, with the management's permission, he goes from box to box, while the candles are being extinguished, picking up the lost pins. Not a single one escapes his mouse's eyes, no matter where it lies, and in that twinkling when the attendant is extinguishing the last candle, our farmer seizes the last pin, saying, "Thank goodness! Tomorrow I will not die of hunger," and runs off with his packet to the shopkeeper.

I visited the Mazarin Library. As I was looking at the rows of books, not knowing which way to go, an old man came up to me and asked, "Would you like to see the noteworthy books and manuscripts?"

"I certainly would, sir," I replied.

"I am at your service," said the old man, as he pointed out to me the rare editions and ancient manuscripts, talking and explaining without interruption. I took him to be the librarian, but this was not so. He has served there for thirty years as a "living catalogue" for those who read and love books. The directors of the Mazarin Library permit the old man to look after the library, and in this way he earns his living. You may give him an *écu* or a copper kopeck — he will accept either with equal gratitude. He will not say, "Too little!" He will not frown. Likewise, for a handful of silver money he will bow no lower to you than usual.

The Parisian beggar wants to look like a noble. He accepts alms without shame, but for an angry word he will challenge you to a duel. He carries a sword!

Paris, June 1790

Let me tell you something about the National Assembly of Paris, about which so much is now appearing in the newspapers. I went there for the first time after dinner. Being unfamiliar with the place, I tried to enter the great door along with the deputies. I was stopped by a sentry, however, who refused to yield to my entreaties. Irritated, I was on the point of returning home, when suddenly a very unattractive man in a dark caftan appeared, seized my hand, and saying, "Allons, Monsieur, allons!" conducted me into the hall.

I took in everything at a single glance: the large gallery; the president's table with two others alongside it for the secretaries; the tribune opposite and tiers of benches all around; and above this, the spectators' boxes.

The session had not yet opened. The place was crowded with people, most of them quite slovenly, their hair disheveled, and wearing surtouts. For about an hour there was much noise and laughter. The spectators clapped their hands to show their impatience. Finally, the very man[13] who had led me in walked up to the president's table, seized a bell, and rang it. All the people began running to their seats, shouting, "To the seats! To the seats!" Only I remained in the middle of the hall. Considering what to do, I sat down on the nearest bench, but a minute later the master of ceremonies, a man in a black coat, came up to me and said, "You cannot stay here!" I rose and changed to another place.

Meanwhile, one of the members, M. André, was reading a recommendation of the War Commission. Everyone listened to him attentively. I was attentive, too, but not for long, because the cursed black coat flew up to me again and said, "Sir, you must know that only members are permitted in this hall."

"Where am I to go then?"

"Go to the boxes."

"And if there is no room there?"

[13] He was Rabaut [de] Saint-Étienne. — N.K.

"Then go home or wherever you like." I left. But the next time I went there I sat in a box for five or six hours and witnessed one of the stormiest sessions. Deputies of the clergy offered a proposal that the Catholic religion be acknowledged the only or established religion in France. Mirabeau passionately disputed this.

"From this spot," said he, "I see the very window from which the son of Catherine de Médicis [Charles IX] shot the Protestants."

Abbé Maury jumped up from his seat and shouted, "Nonsense! You cannot see it from here."

The deputies and spectators roared with laughter. Such improprieties occur very often. In general the sessions are conducted with little solemnity and no pomp whatsoever, although many of the orators speak fluently. Mirabeau and Maury are always in single combat, like Achilles and Hector.

The day after the debates about the Catholic religion, paper snuffboxes *à l'Abbé Maury* appeared in the shops. When you opened the lid, out jumped an abbé. Such are the French. They have some contrivance to suit every occasion.

Let me tell you another anecdote of this nature. On the day that the Assembly decided to issue assignats I was at the theater. They performed an old opera of a shoemaker, who, in the second act, was supposed to sing a certain *vaudeville.* But instead, he sang new verses in praise of the king and the National Assembly with this refrain:

L'argent caché ressortira
Par le moyen des assignats.
[Hidden money will appear again
By means of the assignats.]

The spectators were beside themselves with delight and made the actor repeat ten times, "L'argent caché ressortira."

It seemed to them that heaps of gold were already lying before them!...

Paris, June 1790

...I have left you, dear Paris, left you with regret and gratitude! I lived amid your tumultuous happenings serenely and cheerfully, like a carefree citizen of the world. I viewed your unrest with the tranquil soul of a peaceful shepherd viewing the stormy sea from a mountain. Neither your Jacobins nor your Aristocrats caused me any harm. I listened to the disputes without disputing. To delight my eyes and ears, I visited your beautiful temples, where the flashing God of the Arts emits rays of the intellect and the talents, where the Genius of Fame rests majestically on its laurels!

Although I have been unable to describe all the pleasant impressions you made on me, and to avail myself of everything, yet I do not leave you with an empty soul. There remain ideas and memories! Perhaps sometime I shall visit you again and shall compare the past with the present. Perhaps then I shall enjoy you even more in my greater maturity of judgment, or sigh with regret over my lost vitality or feeling.

With what delight would I once more ascend Mont Valérien, from which my eyes so often darted through your picturesque surroundings! With what delight, seated in the shade of the Bois de Boulogne, would I once again unroll the scroll of history[14] to find in it a prophecy of the future!

[14] In the Bois de Boulogne I read Abbé de Mably's *History of the French Government.* — N.K.

Perhaps then all that is obscure will become clarified. Perhaps then I shall love mankind still more or, having closed the scroll, shall cease being concerned over his fate.

Farewell, dear Paris! Farewell, dear B__!

Finally, permit me to say to you, my friends, that, except for my usual melancholy moments, I have known nothing in Paris but pleasure. To pass about four months there is, in the words of a certain English doctor, to wheedle a very rich gift out of the niggardly enchantress, Fate. Almost all my countrymen accompanied me, as well as B__ and Baron B__. We embraced several times before I took my place in the diligence.

Now we are spending the night about thirty versts[15] from Paris. My soul is so occupied with what has passed that my imagination has not yet once glanced into the future. I am going to England, and I still do not think about it.

[15] About twenty English miles.

APPENDIX

THE SIZE AND POPULATION OF PARIS (14TH—18TH CENTURIES)

The changing topographical limits of Paris during the centuries covered by this book are very well understood and will be discussed below. But the size of the city's population during this period is much more difficult to ascertain. Some of our writers commented on the extent of population. The Venetian secretary (1577–79) wrote that "according to common opinion there are continually in this city more than one million persons." But he immediately qualified this statement by adding that "[t]he number is however impossible to know in a precise manner, not only because of the great multitude of foreigners who come and go every day, but because the inhabitants themselves (I mean the common people) change their dwellings every three months, so that one cannot keep an accurate register of them." He gave the university population as rarely less than 30,000 students. More than a hundred years later, in 1692, Marana offered one million as the size of the population. And in 1790, Karamzin specified 1,130,450 inhabitants, including 150,000 foreigners and 200,000 servants, "according to the latest calculation."

Karamzin did not cite the source of his figures, but if we subtract the foreigners and servants (the latter class officially barred from active citizenry in September 1789), Paris's population in 1790 was 780,450, rather far from the million persons reported in earlier centuries by the Venetian secretary and by Marana. But Karamzin could not have gleaned his figures from an official census, for none was taken until 1796, and this put the population at 556,304. But the actual population was larger, because the census excluded servants, foreigners, students, beggars, the underworld, and other "floating" groups or those living on the margins of society.

Five hundred fifty-six thousand three hundred and four "official" inhabitants in 1796 — this is our earliest, secure figure with which to survey and gauge earlier estimates of the Parisian population.

In 1323, when Jean de Jandun wrote his "Treatise," Paris lay within the walls erected under Philip Augustus from 1190 to 1212. Included were the Île de la Cité, the western part of the Île Notre-Dame (later the Île Saint-Louis), and areas on the Right and Left Banks. On the Left Bank, Jean de Jandun's Paris was delimited at the east by the present Rue des Fossés Saint-Bernard and Rue du Cardinal Lemoine, at the west by the Rues Monsieur Le Prince, de l'Ancienne Comédie, and Mazarine. The southernmost limit of the Left Bank was in the vicinity of the present Panthéon. On the Right Bank, the city's ramparts reached at the east to the present Rues des Jardins-Saint-Paul and de Sévigné in the Marais, at the west to the Rue de l'Oratoire at the Louvre; the northernmost limit followed the Rue Étienne-Marcel.

In 1328, just five years later, the new king, Philip VI (1328–50), ordered a census of the number of hearths (*feux*) in his realm, for the purpose of levying a tax to pay for his wars. A hearth was a family possessing a common fireplace, the definition of a place of habitation (*foyer*). The census listed 61,098 hearths in Paris. The problem for demographers is to determine how many persons on average composed a *foyer*. Depending on this figure, estimates for the city's population in 1328 range from 80,000 to 240,000, with most modern analysts opting for somewhat more than 200,000. This figure means that Paris in the fourteenth century was by far the most populous city in Europe.

By the early fifteenth century, the time of Guillebert de Mets, the Right Bank had been expanded under Charles V and Charles VI (new walls built 1365–95). The rampart now followed a trajectory marked (beginning at the west) by the present Pyramide du Louvre, the Place du Théâtre-Français, the Jardin du Palais-Royal, then northeast along the Rue d'Aboukir to approximatively the level of the Grands Boulevards, following their route eastward and then southeastward, down the Boulevard Bourdon to the Seine. The Left Bank remained defined by the wall of Philip Augustus. To a city occupying 272 hectares (672.13 acres), Charles V and his successor had added 167 hectares (412.66 acres) on the Right Bank alone, thus creating a walled area of 439 hectares (1084.79 acres).

What was the population in the early fifteenth century? We know that the Black Death had decimated Paris in 1348 and 1349, but the population had recovered by 1400, probably to its early fourteenth-century size. But the grave political troubles which afflicted the city from 1407 on,[1] compounded by epidemics,[2] led to a significant exodus and

[1]See above, p. 23

[2]See above, pp. 23, 37.

loss of inhabitants, and surviving fiscal registers of 1421–23 suggest a population that had shrunk to 80,000–100,000.

By 1500 the Parisian population had again recovered its early-fourteenth century level. A strong demographic growth ensued, so that by the beginning of the reign of Charles IX (1560–74) there were around 350,000 inhabitants, by modern estimation. This figure was reduced by the effect of the Wars of Religion and disease, so that when Lippomano and his secretary were in Paris (1577–79), the population stood at perhaps 300,000, not the million reported by the secretary. But, beginning in 1566, the area of the walled metropolis was increased to 567 hectares (1401.10 acres) by the erection of new ramparts at the western end of the Right Bank, reaching from the site of the later Place de la Concorde northward to the line of the later Grands Boulevards, and rejoining the wall of Charles V at the Porte Saint-Denis. Paris was still Europe's most populous city.

In the seventeenth century, the population experienced a significant expansion, and the old walls were torn down, replaced by boulevards. By the time of Marana's "Letter" (1692) — late in the reign of Louis XIV — Paris is estimated to have had 400–500,000 inhabitants. A century later, the census of 1796 revealed a city of 556,304, marking considerable growth if we accept the lower figure, only a moderate increase using the higher one. But by now Paris had been surpassed by London, where around 1700 there were already some 575,000 people, a figure that ballooned to about 960,000 by 1801. But Paris remained the most populous metropolis on the Continent.

However, the area of Paris in 1790, when Karamzin visited the city, was significantly larger than in Marana's day, although it had again been enclosed within a wall! This was the wall of the Farmers General (built mainly 1784–87, finished in 1790), which was punctuated by small pavilions where taxes on goods entering the city were collected.[1] The wall enclosed the faubourgs which had grown up all around the city, and included much open or sparsely-developed land. On the Right Bank, the area enclosed half of the present 12th Arrondissement, all of the 11th, 10th, 9th, 8th, and part of the 16th. On the Left Bank, the wall encompassed the northern parts of the present 13th, 14th, and 15th Arrondissements.

For a concise discussion of the population of Paris through the ages, see Jean Favier, *Paris: deux milles ans d'histoire* (Paris: Fayard, 1997), 37–66.

[1] Karamzin admired the architecture of one of these; see above, p. 108.

Map 1. Paris c. 1400

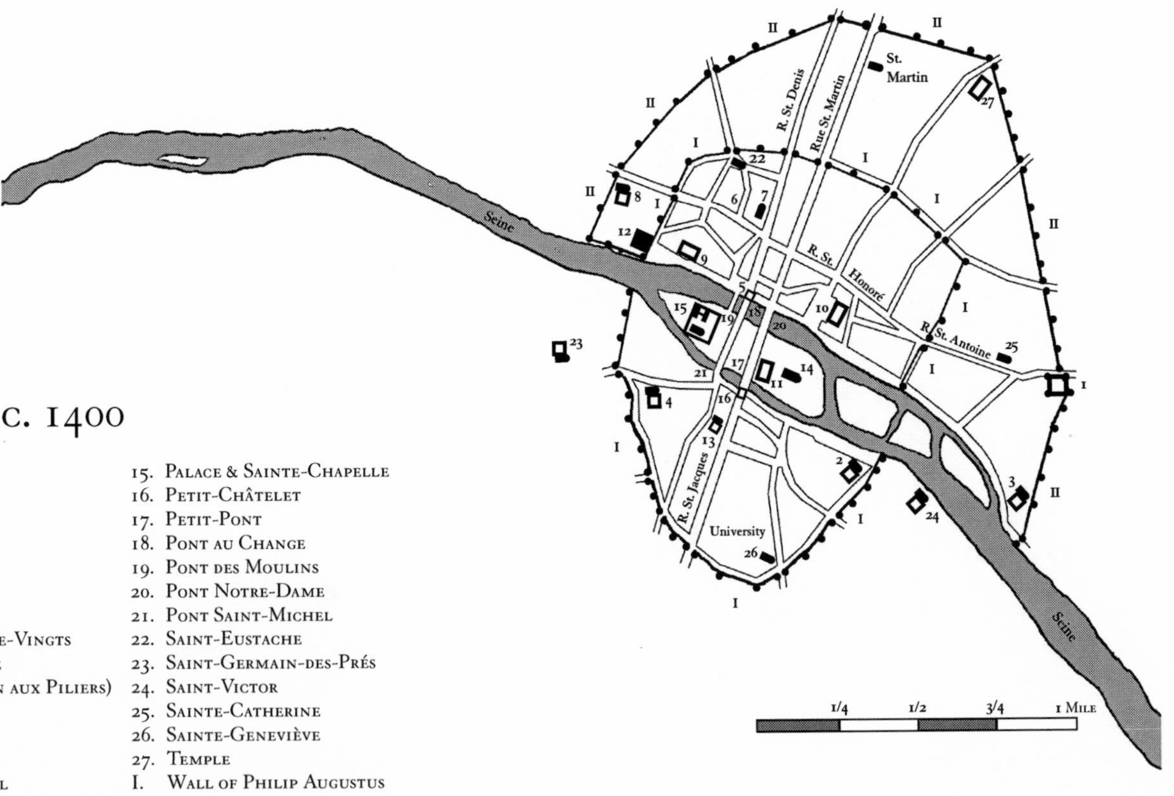

1. Bastille
2. Bernardins
3. Célestins
4. Cordeliers
5. Grand-Châtelet
6. Halles des Champeaux
7. Holy Innocents
8. Hospital of the Quinze-Vingts
9. Hôtel de For-L'Evêque
10. Hôtel de Ville (Maison aux Piliers)
11. Hôtel-Dieu
12. Louvre
13. Mathurins
14. Notre-Dame Cathedral
15. Palace & Sainte-Chapelle
16. Petit-Châtelet
17. Petit-Pont
18. Pont au Change
19. Pont des Moulins
20. Pont Notre-Dame
21. Pont Saint-Michel
22. Saint-Eustache
23. Saint-Germain-des-Prés
24. Saint-Victor
25. Sainte-Catherine
26. Sainte-Geneviève
27. Temple

I. Wall of Philip Augustus
II. Wall of Charles V

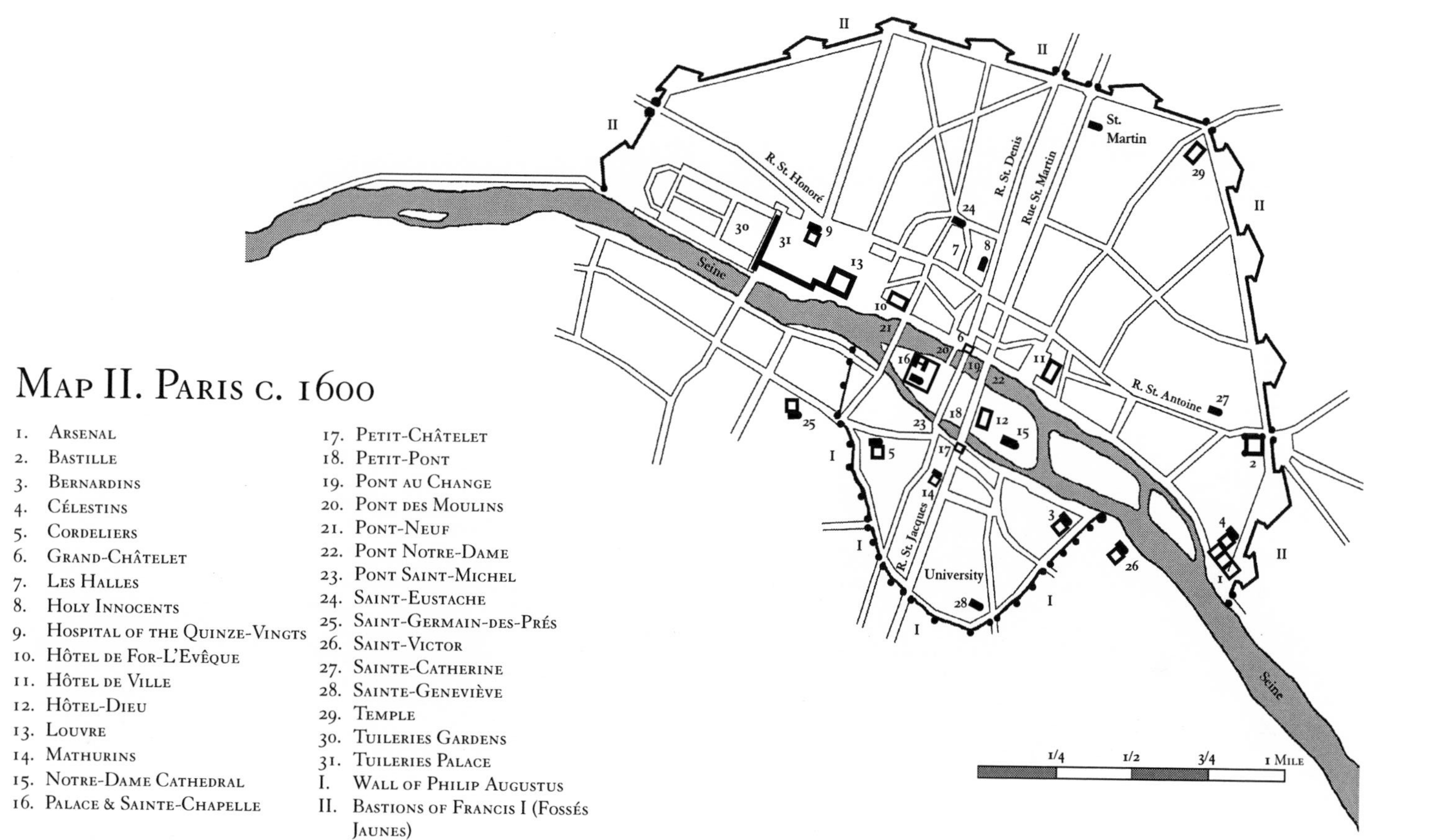

Map II. Paris c. 1600

1. Arsenal
2. Bastille
3. Bernardins
4. Célestins
5. Cordeliers
6. Grand-Châtelet
7. Les Halles
8. Holy Innocents
9. Hospital of the Quinze-Vingts
10. Hôtel de For-L'Evêque
11. Hôtel de Ville
12. Hôtel-Dieu
13. Louvre
14. Mathurins
15. Notre-Dame Cathedral
16. Palace & Sainte-Chapelle
17. Petit-Châtelet
18. Petit-Pont
19. Pont au Change
20. Pont des Moulins
21. Pont-Neuf
22. Pont Notre-Dame
23. Pont Saint-Michel
24. Saint-Eustache
25. Saint-Germain-des-Prés
26. Saint-Victor
27. Sainte-Catherine
28. Sainte-Geneviève
29. Temple
30. Tuileries Gardens
31. Tuileries Palace

I. Wall of Philip Augustus
II. Bastions of Francis I (Fossés Jaunes)

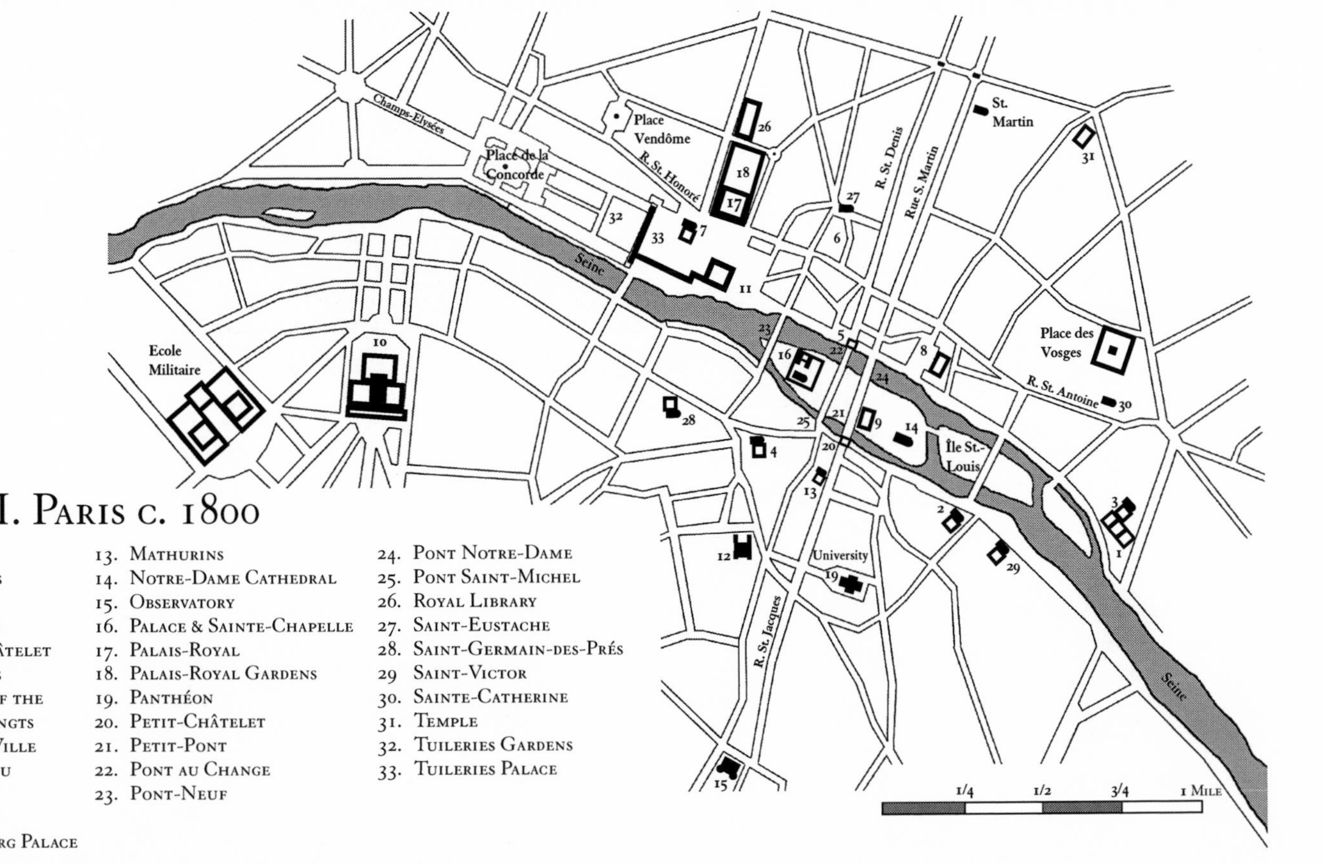

Map III. Paris c. 1800

1. Arsenal
2. Bernardins
3. Célestins
4. Cordeliers
5. Grand-Châtelet
6. Les Halles
7. Hospital of the Quinze-Vingts
8. Hôtel de Ville
9. Hôtel-Dieu
10. Invalides
11. Louvre
12. Luxembourg Palace & Garden
13. Mathurins
14. Notre-Dame Cathedral
15. Observatory
16. Palace & Sainte-Chapelle
17. Palais-Royal
18. Palais-Royal Gardens
19. Panthéon
20. Petit-Châtelet
21. Petit-Pont
22. Pont au Change
23. Pont-Neuf
24. Pont Notre-Dame
25. Pont Saint-Michel
26. Royal Library
27. Saint-Eustache
28. Saint-Germain-des-Prés
29 Saint-Victor
30. Sainte-Catherine
31. Temple
32. Tuileries Gardens
33. Tuileries Palace

Parisian History, Urbanism and Architecture: A Select Bibliography

The best one-volume histories of Paris are Marcel Le Clère, ed., *Paris de la Préhistoire à nos jours* (Saint-Jean-d'Angély: Editions Bordessoules, 1985) and Jean Favier, *Paris: deux milles ans d'histoire* (Paris: Fayard, 1997). Le Clère's volume is especially useful for its quotations from source documents, illustrations, and maps. Comprehensive histories in English are surprisingly few: Thomas Okey, *Paris and Its Story* (London: Dent, 1904) is dated, and Robert Cole's concise *A Traveller's History of Paris*, 2d ed. (New York: Interlink Books, 1998) should be used with caution.

The most scholarly and detailed modern histories of the city are found in the multi-volume series, "Nouvelle Histoire de Paris." The volumes which cover the timespan of this book are: Raymond Cazelles, *De la fin du règne de Philippe Auguste à la mort de Charles V* (Paris: Hachette, 1972); Jean Favier, *Paris au XVe siècle, 1380–1500* (Paris: Hachette, 1974); Jean-Pierre Babelon, *Paris au XVIe siècle* (Paris: Hachette, 1986); René Pillorget, *Paris sous les premiers Bourbons* (Paris: Hachette, 1988); Georges Dethan, *Paris au temps de Louis XIV, 1660–1715* (Paris: Hachette, 1990); Jean Chagniot, *Paris au XVIIIe siècle* (Paris, Hachette, 1988); Marcel R. Reinhard, *La Révolution, 1789–1799* (Paris: Hachette, 1971).

In Old Paris

For the development of the physical city, see Pierre Lavedan, *Histoire de l'urbanisme à Paris,* 2d ed., Nouvelle Histoire de Paris (Paris: Hachette, 1993). The best historical survey of Parisian architecture is Dieter Kimpel, *Paris: Führer durch die Stadtbaugeschichte* (Munich: Hirmer Verlag, 1982); this includes discussions of architectural sculpture. Individual (mostly extant) buildings are catalogued in Jean-Marie Pérouse de Montclos, ed., *Paris,* Le guide du patrimoine (Paris: Hachette, 1994). A street-by-street survey, which includes material on vanished features, is Jacques Hillairet, *Dictionnaire historique des rues de Paris,* 2d ed. (Paris: Les Editions du Minuit, 1963), 2 vols.

ARCHITECTURAL GAZETTEER[1]

*ARSENAL. The Arsenal, which the Venetian secretary saw in the 1570s, was a modest affair, consisting of two barn-like structures that had been used by Francis I since 1533 for the casting of cannon and appropriated for the Crown by Henry II in 1547 as the Arsenal du Roi or Grand Arsenal. It was located on the Right Bank along the Seine, at the eastern end of the city, between the present Rue de Petit-Musc and Boulevard Bourdon.

*BASTILLE. A small towered fortress begun under Charles V in 1370 and finished c. 1382 under Charles VI. It protected the eastern end of Paris. Used occasionally as a prison since the fifteenth century, it became exclusively one (for aristocratic prisoners) from the time of Richelieu until its demolition in 1789 at the start of the Revolution. Its site occupied the western side of the Place de la Bastille and the beginning of the Rue Saint-Antoine (Right Bank).

*BERNARDINS. A college for the instruction of Cistercian monks, founded in 1245 by Étienne de Lexington and rebuilt from 1338 on with the patronage of Pope Benedict XII and Cardinal Guillaume Curti. It included its own church and dormitories. The Bernardins occupied a large area in the Latin Quarter, with its entrance on the Rue des Bernardins. The huge vaulted refectory, sacristy, and cellar have survived.

[1]Architectural features that are merely mentioned in the text are not discussed here. Destroyed buildings are indicated by an asterisk (*).

*CÉLESTINS. A Benedictine monastery founded by Charles V in 1365. It occupied an area on the Right Bank between the Rue du Petit-Musc and the Rue de l'Arsenal.

*CHÂTELET. The Grand Châtelet stood on the Right Bank at the entrance to the PONT AU CHANGE (Grand-Pont), its main façade facing the Rue Saint-Denis. It was a towered fort — built in 1130 and successively enlarged over the centuries — which served as the seat and residence of the royal provost of Paris, who exercised military, financial, and judicial powers. The building contained a prison and morgue. (See also PETIT-CHÂTELET.)

*COLLEGE OF THE BERNARDINS (see BERNARDINS).

*CORDELIERS. A Franciscan monastery founded c. 1230. It was an important school of theology and philosophy in the Middle Ages. The monastery formerly stood in the Latin Quarter, on the site now occupied by the École Pratique de Médecine and the Lycée Saint-Louis. The refectory (14th–16th centuries) is extant (entrance 15, Rue de l'École-de-Médecine).

*GRAND-PONT (see PONT AU CHANGE).

*HALLES DES CHAMPEAUX. The central market of Paris, built in 1183 by Philip II Augustus on the Right Bank. Covered sheds were constructed within a walled enclosure, and food as well as all types of merchandise were sold there. It was the precursor of the later Halles Centrales.

*HOLY INNOCENTS (LES SAINTS-INNOCENTS): CEMETERY AND CHURCH. This was the main cemetery of Paris until its destruction in the late eighteenth century. It occupied an area in the heart of the Right Bank, between the Rue Saint-Denis and LES HALLES. A burial site since Merovingian times, it was enclosed by a wall by Philip II Augustus c. 1186. The church, on its east side, was probably built in the early thirteenth century and enlarged in the fifteenth. It housed as a relic a Christian child (the Innocent) allegedly killed by the Jews. The cemetery was surrounded by charnel houses, and within the arcades was a famous fresco cycle of the Danse Macabre (early 15th century).

*HOSPITAL OF THE QUINZE-VINGTS. A hospice rather than a hospital, this institution was founded by Louis IX in 1254–61 for the housing of 300 blind people (*quinze-vingts* = fifteen score). It was built outside the rampart of Philip Augustus in the Faubourg Saint-Honoré on the Right Bank, but when Marana wrote of it in 1692 it was well within the seventeenth-century city (approximately at 155, Rue Saint-Honoré).

*HÔTEL DE BEAUMARCHAIS. Built in 1790 for the famous playwright Pierre-Augustin Caron de Beaumarchais; the architect was Paul-Guillaume Lemoine. The entrance was formerly at 2, Boulevard Beaumarchais (Right Bank). The hôtel was under construction at the time of Karamzin's visit.

*HÔTEL-DIEU. The general hospital of Paris, begun 1165 on the initiative of King Philip II Augustus and Bishop Maurice de Sully; it was largely complete by c. 1255, thanks to the patronage of Louis IX (Saint Louis) and his mother, Blanche of Castile. All types of maladies were treated here except contagious diseases, which were treated in more outlying hospitals. The Hôtel-Dieu stood on the south side of the Île de la Cité, near NOTRE-DAME.

*HÔTEL DE FOR-L'EVÊQUE. Built in 1222, this building belonged to the bishop of Paris until 1674, serving as a prison for those whose cases fell within the bishop's jurisdiction. Guillebert de Mets reported that temporal cases were heard there. The small building formerly stood at 19, Rue Saint-Germain-l'Auxerrois, between that street and the Quai de la Mégisserie (formerly the Rue de l'École-Saint-Germain) on the Right Bank.

*HÔTEL DE GUILLEMIN DE SANGUIN. Known only by the brief description by Guillebert de Mets. The Rue des Bourdonnais still exists on the Right Bank.

*HÔTEL DE JACQUES DUCHIÉ. Known only by the long description by Guillebert de Mets. A fragment of the Rue de Prouvelles survives on the Right Bank as the Rue des Prouvaires.

*HÔTEL DU SIEUR MILLE BAILLET. Known only by the brief description by Guillebert de Mets. The Rue de la Verrerie still exists on the Right Bank.

*HÔTEL DE VILLE. The site of the Hôtel de Ville was the east side of the Place de Grève (now Place de l'Hôtel de Ville) on the Right Bank along the Seine. This square served as a small port and site of economic activity; it was also the main theater for public executions. In 1357 the corporation of Parisian merchants — a powerful body, headed by the provost of merchants, which effectively administered the city along with the royal provost (see CHÂTELET) — moved to a small building on the Place de Grève called the *Maison aux Piliers. Here the corporation had its headquarters until 1533, when, at the instigation of Francis I, a new building was begun — the Hôtel de Ville or Town Hall — designed in Renaissance style by an Italian architect, Domenico da Cortona. This structure, completed in the early seventeenth century, was destroyed in 1871 and replaced by the present pastiche.

INVALIDES. This huge complex was commissioned by Louis XIV as a home for his war veterans. The Hôtel itself, in which the veterans were housed, was designed by Libéral Bruant and begun in 1671. Bruant was supplanted by Jules Hardouin-Mansart, the architect of the Soldiers' Church (built 1677–79) and the central-plan Dôme (built 1678–1706). The Invalides still stands on the Left Bank, between the Esplanade des Invalides and the Avenue de Tourville.

LOUVRE. Begun under Philip Augustus in the 1190s as a fortress on the Right Bank protecting the western approaches to the medieval city, the Louvre was transformed into a luxurious residence c. 1360 by Charles V. From that time on it started to replace the PALACE on the Île de la Cité as the principal royal Parisian seat. Its central tower was razed in 1528 by Francis I, a signal of his intention to refashion the whole into a Renaissance palace. Work following the designs of Pierre Lescot began in 1546 and was continued by Henry II. A long gallery (Galerie du Bord de l'Eau) linking the Louvre and TUILERIES was built under Henry IV (1595–1608). The east façade or colonnade (greatly admired by Karamzin), designed and begun in 1667, was the work of a committee (Louis Le Vau, Charles Le Brun, Claude Perrault).

LUXEMBOURG PALACE AND GARDEN. The Luxembourg was begun in 1615 for Marie de Médicis, widow of Henry IV; the architect was Salomon de Brosse. The palace and garden were probably meant to recall the Palazzo Pitti in Florence, where Marie had spent her early years. A public museum from 1750 to 1779, it apparently could still be freely visited at the end of the eighteenth century, as attested by Karamzin's visit (its greatest attraction was Rubens's *Life of Marie de Médicis* cycle, now in the LOUVRE). The palace (now the French Senate) and garden are located on the Left Bank, within a large precinct bordered by the Rue de Vaugirard, the Rues Guynemer and Auguste Comte, and the Boulevard Saint-Michel. Now the heart of the Left Bank, the area in the seventeenth century was at a remove from the denser quarters, giving the Luxembourg the air of a suburban villa.

*MAISON AUX PILIERS (see HÔTEL DE VILLE).

*MATHURINS. The small monastery and church of the Mathurins stood in the Latin Quarter, near the Hôtel (now Musée) de Cluny. There were housed the monks of the Order of the Holy Trinity and Redemption of Captives (called Mathurins), who had been invited to Paris in 1229.

NOTRE-DAME CATHEDRAL. Located at the eastern end of the Île de la Cité, Notre-Dame was begun in 1163 under Bishop Maurice de Sully and finished c. 1345 after a series of building campaigns. It is a major work of High Gothic style, richly decorated with sculpture and stained glass. To the south stood the *Bishop's Palace (12th century), to the north thirty-seven *houses occupied by the canons of the cathedral.

OBSERVATORY (OBSERVATOIRE). Commissioned by Louis XIV as a royal observatory, this structure was designed by Claude Perrault and begun in 1667. Astronomical observations and scientific experiments were conducted here. It still stands on the Left Bank at the south end of the Avenue de l'Observatoire.

PALACE (PALAIS). Originally the royal palace, on the western end of the Île de la Cité. The palace was developed from the early eleventh century on and reconstructed under King Philip the Fair (1268–1314). It housed apartments for the king, the royal family, and entourage, as well as royal administrative offices, like the Chambre des Comptes (exchequer). It was also the seat of the Parlement (law court), and luxury goods and books were sold there. Famous features included the Great Hall (Grand'Salle), with its statues of the French kings and a huge marble table used for banqueting and public announcements. The SAINTE-CHAPELLE, the king's private chapel built under Louis IX, was within the precinct of the palace. After Charles V renovated the LOUVRE c. 1360, it replaced the Palace as the royal residence in Paris. Extant vestiges of the Palace are within a section of the modern Palais de Justice known as the Conciergerie. They include several towers of the north perimeter wall, the Salle des Gardes, the Salle des Gens d'Armes, and the kitchens.

PALAIS-ROYAL. Initially constructed for Cardinal Richelieu in 1624–36 by Jacques Lemercier and known as the Palais-Cardinal, the building passed to the Crown in 1642, changing its name to the Palais-Royal. In 1692 it was given by Louis XIV to the Orléans branch of the royal family. It was partially burned in 1763 and subsequently underwent numerous remodelings. The façade of the palace fronts the Place du Palais-Royal, on the Right Bank near the LOUVRE. The public garden, extending behind the building to the north between the Rue de Montpensier and the Rue de Valois, was enclosed 1781–84 on three sides by the architect Victor Louis with uniform ranges of buildings consisting of arcaded galleries with shops and cafés on the ground floor and apartments above.

*PETIT-CHÂTELET. A small fort that stood on the Left Bank at the entrance of the PETIT-PONT. Built in stone in 1369, it was used as a prison from 1398 on, under the control of the royal provost of Paris. (See also CHÂTELET.)

*PETIT-PONT. Built in stone after the floods of 1296, it was on the site of the present Petit-Pont, linking the Left Bank with the Île de la Cité. It was lined with houses and shops and was guarded by the PETIT-CHÂTELET. Taxes on food and merchandise were collected here.

PLACE DE GRÈVE (see HÔTEL DE VILLE).

*PONT AU CHANGE. Constructed after 1296 and finished in 1305, it was called the Grand-Pont or Pont-du-Roy until the end of the fourteenth century. Its houses and shops were occupied by money-changers and goldsmiths. It was protected by the CHÂTELET. It occupied the site of the present Pont au Change, linking the Right Bank and the Île de la Cité.

*PONT DES MOULINS. Built just west of the PONT AU CHANGE after 1296, this wooden bridge (also known as the Pont aux Meuniers) was for the emplacement of water-mills, which operated millstones. The mills were owned by the chapter of NOTRE-DAME. The Venetian secretary reported shops on the bridge in the 1570s.

PONT-NEUF. Built mainly from 1599 to 1606, it was the first Parisian bridge without houses and shops. It connects the Right and Left Banks via the tip of the western point of the Île de la Cité. The Venetian secretary mentions an early project for the bridge, recorded in an anonymous painting in the Musée Carnavalet, Paris.

*PONT NOTRE-DAME. Built beginning in 1413. It was lined with houses and shops and connected the Right Bank and the Île de la Cité. The bridge collapsed in 1499 and was reconstructed at the beginning of the sixteenth century by the Italian engineer Fra Giovanni Giocondo. It occupied the site of the present Pont Notre-Dame.

*PONT SAINT-MICHEL. Built originally in 1378 and lined with houses and shops, it connected the Left Bank with the Île de la Cité. It occupied the site of the modern Pont Saint-Michel.

*ROYAL LIBRARY (BIBLIOTHÈQUE ROYALE). A decisive step in the formation of the Royal Library was taken in 1666, when Colbert established the collection in a house in the Rue Vivienne on the Right Bank. Beginning in 1724, the library was moved across the street to the Hôtel de Nevers, which was enlarged in the course of the eighteenth century. When Karamzin visited the library in 1790, it occupied the entire site where the nineteenth-century Bibliothèque Nationale was later built, immediately to the north of the garden of the PALAIS-ROYAL on the Right Bank. Scholars were granted access to these libraries from the start; the general public was freely admitted from 1692 on.

SAINT-EUSTACHE. This church was begun in 1532 and not consecrated until 1637, serving as the parish church of the HALLES quarter on the Right Bank. The architect is unknown. Built to the plan of NOTRE-DAME and on the same scale, it combines Gothic space and vaulting with Renaissance articulation. The church stands at 2, Rue du Jour.

SAINT-GERMAIN-DES-PRÉS. An abbey church on the Left Bank, dating from the tenth to the twelfth centuries, and built in Romanesque style. The abbey formerly owned extensive land on the Left Bank, hence its appellation "des prés" (of the meadows). It is extant at Place Saint-Germain-des-Prés.

*SAINT-VICTOR. A great Augustinian abbey founded in 1113 by Louis VI the Fat. A famous school developed there in the Middle Ages. The abbey was built in the Faubourg Saint-Victor on the Left Bank, approximately on the site of the present University of Paris VI–VII, between Place Jussieu and the Quai Saint-Bernard.

*SAINTE-CATHERINE [-du-Val-des-Ecoliers]. This priory church was finished in 1229. It stood in the Marais, on the site of the present Marché Sainte-Catherine.

SAINTE-CHAPELLE. Built in 1242–48 for King Louis IX (Saint Louis) as part of the PALACE on the Île de la Cité. It consists of two superposed chapels. The lower chapel was for the king's servants and the inhabitants of the Palace; the upper chapel — the masterpiece of Rayonnant Gothic style with remarkable walls of stained-glass — was for the use of the king and his immediate entourage. The Sainte-Chapelle housed the holiest relics in France, first and foremost the Crown of Thorns. It is now within the precinct of the Palais de Justice and can be reached at 4, Boulevard du Palais.

*SAINTE-GENEVIÈVE (medieval). The medieval abbey church (rebuilt 11th–13th centuries in Romanesque style) stood on the Montagne Sainte-Geneviève on the Left Bank. The church housed the body of Saint Geneviève, the patroness of Paris, in a reliquary chest, which was carried in procession through the streets in times of need. In the choir were the tombs of Clovis, the first Christian king of France, and his wife, Queen Clotilde. Only the bell-tower (the

"Tower of Clovis," 12th–15th centuries) still exists, within the perimeter of the Lycée Henri-IV (23, Rue Clovis).

SAINTE-GENEVIÈVE (= Panthéon). Karamzin saw the successor church, commissioned by Louis XV and designed by Jacques-Germain Soufflot, whose earliest project dates from 1757; construction began in 1764 and was finished in 1790, when Karamzin was in Paris. The structure was designed in a radically new, neo-classical style. The building was secularized the next year during the French Revolution and re-named the Panthéon. Subsequently modified, it stands on the Place du Panthéon.

*TEMPLE. The name given to the Parisian home of the Knights of the Temple (Templars), a religious military order founded in 1120. The Templars arrived in Paris in 1139, later moving (c. 1240) to an area on the Right Bank far from the center, now bounded by the Rues du Temple, de Bretagne, de Picardie, and Béranger. Within the towered, walled enclosure were the palace of the grand prior, monastic buildings, a church (of typically round form), hospital, cemetery, prison, and a huge tower or keep. The knights were entrusted with the royal treasure from 1190 on, when Philip Augustus went on crusade, and continued to serve as royal bankers until the entire, international order was dissolved in the early fourteenth century. All Templar property was turned over to the Knights of Saint John of Jerusalem (Hospitalers), a rival order, who were still occupying the Temple when the Venetian secretary saw it in the 1570s.

TUILERIES. The *palace, erected on the Right Bank west of the LOUVRE, was begun in 1564 as a suburban villa for the queen-mother, Catherine de Médicis, widow of Henry II.

The original architect was Philibert de l'Orme; the building was gradually completed in the later sixteenth and seventeenth centuries by other architects. It was linked to the Louvre by a long gallery (Galerie du Bord de l'Eau) built under Henry IV. The garden was also begun in 1564 and opened to the public in the early seventeenth century, serving as a fashionable green space throughout the Old Regime; it was remodeled between 1664 and 1680 by André Le Nôtre.

UNIVERSITY. The University of Paris developed from the monastic school of NOTRE-DAME and received official recognition in the early thirteenth century from king and pope. It consisted of a collection of schools in the Latin Quarter on the Left Bank, the most famous being the Collège de Sorbonne (founded 1257) and the Collège de Navarre (founded 1304). In the Middle Ages it was the largest and most prestigious university in Europe, with an international student body and faculty. None of the medieval buildings have survived.

GLOSSARY[1]

ACHILLES: The greatest Greek warrior, hero of Homer's *Iliad.*

AMINTA: The shepherd–protagonist of Torquato Tasso's pastoral drama of the same name (1573).

ARCHIMEDES: Greek mathematician, astronomer, and inventor (c. 287–12 B.C.E.).

ARMIDA: A beautiful sorceress in Torquato Tasso's *Jerusalem Delivered* (published 1581). Her garden was a realm of sensual delights.

ATREUS: In Greek mythology, a rival, along with his brother Thyestes, for the throne of Mycenae. The story was dramatized by Prosper-Jolyot de Crébillon (*Atrée et Thyeste,* 1707).

BOILEAU: Nicolas Boileau (1636–1711), French literary critic and poet.

CACUS: In classical mythology, a savage monster who stole cattle from HERCULES, who slew him.

CALYPSO: In Homer's *Odyssey,* the nymph of the island of Ogyia, who detained Odysseus for seven years.

CATO: Marcus Porcius Cato, known as Cato the Elder (234–149 B.C.E.), Roman statesman.

CHARLES V: King of France (1364–80).

CHARLES VI: King of France (1380–1422).

[1]Historical figures discussed in the text are not listed here.

CHARYBDIS: In Homer's *Odyssey*, a whirlpool in the Straits of Messina, opposite SCYLLA. Scylla and Charybdis are proverbial dangers.

CHRISTINE DE PISAN: Italian-born proto-feminist French writer (c. 1364–c. 1430), France's first professional female author.

COLOSSUS OF RHODES: A huge statue of Helios, the sun god, on the island of Rhodes. It was sculpted by Chares of Lindos c. 300 B.C.E. One of the Seven Wonders of the ancient world.

CROESUS: King of Lydia (c. 560–46 B.C.E.), fabled for his wealth.

CYRUS: Cyrus the Great, king of Persia (c. 557–30 B.C.E.).

DEMETRIUS: Demetrius I Poliorcetes (336–283 B.C.E.), king of Macedonia (294–87 B.C.E.).

DIOGENES: Greek philosopher (c. 412/403–c.324/321 B.C.E.).

DU GUESCLIN: Bertrand Du Guesclin (c. 1320–80), French soldier and constable of France (1370–80).

ENDYMION: In Greek mythology, a beautiful youth, sometimes a shepherd, beloved by Selene (the Moon).

FLAMEL, NICOLAS: French scribe and alchemist (c. 1330–1418). Guillebert de Mets wrote that "[h]e built several houses in which tradesmen lived downstairs, and the rent that they paid supported poor workmen upstairs" (see above, p. 36). One of these houses survives at 51, Rue de Montmorency, with an inscription dated 1407. This is the oldest surviving house in Paris. His younger brother Jean, also a scribe, died in 1417 or 1418.

FURIES: In Greek mythology, female powers of retribution for wrongs and blood-guilt.

GEBER: Arab alchemist and physician (eighth century; also known as Jabir).

HANNIBAL: Carthaginian general (247 B.C.E.–183/182 B.C.E.).

HECTOR: The greatest of the Trojan warriors. He appears in Homer's *Iliad*.

HENRY III: King of France (1574–89).

HENRY IV: King of France (1589–1610).

HERCULES: In classical mythology, the greatest of the Greek heroes. Among his many adventures was his slavery to Omphale (decreed by Zeus), when he had to dress as a woman and perform women's work, and the theft of his cattle by CACUS, whom he slew.

HESPERIDES: In classical mythology, the daughters of Night who guarded a garden with a tree of golden apples.

ISABELLE (or Isabeau) OF BAVARIA: Wife of CHARLES VI and queen of France from 1385 to 1422; she died in 1435.

JUSTINIAN: Eastern Roman emperor (527–65 C.E.), under whom Roman law was codified and many new laws enacted.

LAÏS: The name of two celebrated Greek courtesans.

LAMIA: A witch in classical mythology.

LAW, JOHN: Scottish financier (1671–1729), whose private French bank was authorized by the French crown in 1716 to issue paper money. An ensuing speculative bubble burst in 1720, and Law fled France.

LIMBOURG BROTHERS: Pol, Herman, and Jean, manuscript illuminators, born after 1385 in Nijmwegen. They reached Paris c. 1400 where they were apprenticed; they later worked for Philip the Bold, duke of Burgundy and John, duke of Berry. They all died in 1416, presumably in an epidemic.

LOUIS IX: King of France (1226–70), canonized in 1297 as Saint Louis.

LOUIS XIV: King of France (1643–1715), known as the Sun King.

LOUIS XVI: King of France (1774–93), executed during the French Revolution.

MARCELLUS: Ulpius Marcellus (mid-second century C.E.), a Roman lawyer.

MARIE-ANTOINETTE: Wife of LOUIS XVI and queen of France (1774–93). She was executed during the French Revolution.

MÉDICIS, CATHERINE DE: Wife of King Henry II and queen of France (1547–59); queen–mother from 1559–89. Mother of HENRY III.

MÉDICIS, MARIE DE: Wife of King HENRY IV and queen of France (1600–1610); queen–mother from 1610–42.

MELPOMENE: Muse of tragedy.

MILO: Greek athlete from Croton (later sixth century B.C.E.).

MIRABEAU: Honoré-Gabriel Riquetti, comte de Mirabeau (1749–91), French revolutionist and statesman.

MOLIÈRE: Professional name of Jean-Baptiste Poquelin (1622–73), French actor and writer of comedies.

MORE, THOMAS: English statesman (1478–1535) and author of *Utopia* (1516). Canonized in 1935.

NECKER, JACQUES: French financier and statesman (1732–1804).

NERO: Roman emperor (54–68 C.E.).

PENELOPE: Wife of Odysseus who, while awaiting his return, pretended to weave a shroud for his father, but which she unravelled every night for ten years.

PENTAPOLIS: The five Greek cities of central Roman Cyrenaica.

PREMIERFAIT, LAURENT DE: French Humanist and translator (1388–1420).

PYTHAGORAS: Greek religious and scientific figure (sixth century B.C.E.). He is said to have introduced the doctrine of the transmigration of souls.

QUEVADO, FRANCISCO DE: Spanish satirist, novelist, and poet (1580–1645).

RINALDO: The hero–knight of Lodovico Ariosto's epic poem *Orlando Furioso* (1516; longer version 1532).

SCIPIO AFRICANUS: Roman general (236–183 B.C.E.) who defeated HANNIBAL at the battle of Zama (202 B.C.E.).

SCYLLA: A fantastic monster who guarded the Straits of Messina, opposite CHARYBDIS (Homer, *Odyssey*).

SENECA: Roman philosopher, dramatist, and tutor of NERO. He was born between 4 B.C.E. and 1 C.E. and committed suicide in 65 C.E.

THALIA: Muse of comedy.

THEMISTOCLES: Athenian politician and general (c. 524–459 B.C.E.).

TOBIAS: In the Apocrypha, the son of Tobit. Sent to collect a loan for his blind father, Tobias, guarded by the archangel Raphael, returned and cured Tobit's blindness with the gall of a fish.

VOLTAIRE: Pen name of François-Marie Arouet (1694–1778), French satirist, philosopher, historian, dramatist, and poet. *Oedipe,* his first tragedy, was cast in its final form in 1717.

XANTHIPPE: The shrewish wife of the Greek philosopher Socrates.

XENOCRATES: Greek philosopher and head of the Platonic Academy in Athens from 339 to 314 B.C.E.

INDEX

G

H

I

J

K

L

M

N

O

P

Q

R

S

This Book Was Completed on December 21, 2001
at Italica Press, New York, New York.
It Was Set in Palatino and
Granjon and Printed on
60 lb Natural Paper
by BookMobile,
St. Paul, MN
U. S. A.
* *
*